# WIDE HORI2

## Hard graft for old-time Fenmen

## "Nothing is certain but uncertainty"

# TREVOR BEVIS

ISBN 0 901680 52 4     COPYRIGHT © T. BEVIS 1994

PUBLISHED BY T. BEVIS B.A., 28 ST. PETER'S ROAD, MARCH, CAMBS. PE15 9NA
Tel: (0354) 57286

PRINTED BY DAVID J. RICHARDS, 1 WEST PARK STREET, CHATTERIS, CAMBS.
PE16 6AH     Tel: (0354) 692947

*The vast openness of the Fens. Where formerly there was marsh bedecked with willow and alder, luxuriant crops grow now.*
*At night transformed into the mysterious sight of will-o'-the-wisps, bright tongues of flame dancing about the gaseous marsh.*
*Water teemed with fish of all kinds ruled by pike and eel, and wildfowl darkened the canopy of limitless sky. The Fenmen, in turn cursed and blessed by nature, accepted harsh terms, but they also enjoyed boundless profit of the four seasons.*

# CONTENTS

ΨΨΨΨΨΨΨΨΨΨΨΨΨΨΨΨΨΨΨΨΨΨΨΨΨΨΨΨ

*Illustrations in this book were selected from Fenland Past and Present
(Miller and Skertchly) published in the nineteenth century; and
Fenland Notes and Queries (edited by Rev. W. D. Sweeting, M.A.),
a series of magazines published between 1900 and 1907.
Other illustrations are by T. Bevis and geographical outlines
are based on old maps.
Grateful acknowledgement to Cambridgeshire County Council Libraries
and Information Service for permission to reproduce relevant
photographs and drawings.*

The River Nene has a turbulent history and was capable of
changing course overnight.  At one time the outfall
of the River Ouse it was always prone to high winds and
abnormally high tides.  This combined natural force was known
as the Aegar, a destructive mixture of elements known thus
in Anglo-Saxon times.  The river was instrumental in
bursting its banks and overflowing thousands of acres of marsh
and land, engulfing Murrow, Newton, Parson Drove and
Leverington and, in the opposite direction, the Walpoles,
Walton, Walsoken and Terrington St. John.  Wisbech and the
"whole of Marshland" were immersed on several occasions.
The illustration shows the Nene outfall, c. 1850.

*(Picture by kind permission of Cambridgeshire County Council Libraries and Information Service)*

# INTRODUCTION

# A little imagination

HAT is all it takes to inject a glimpse of the old-time Fens into receptive minds. The flatness is still there, unchanged from the great level of a thousand years ago, except for the existing myriad of arrow-raight drains and dykes, and the luxuriant fields in place of former vast :panses of water and ancient water courses. The water remains but without ; freedom. Constantly the three-quarter sky which never fails to impress, .d the awareness of prevailing mysteries envelope individuals' minds. nses of freedom and independence are strongest in the Fens, though not great as those experienced by our forefathers.

Here is the soul of a proud people, wrapped in powerful history best scribed as an epic of national proportion, subdued only by the granduer nature in all her moods. Charles Kingsley sensed it and painted a portrait the Fens in these stirring words: "The Fens have a beauty of their own - beauty as of the sea, of boundless expanse and freedom. Overhead the :h of heaven spreads more ample than elsewhere, as over the open sea, .d that vastness gave and still gives such cloud banks, such sunrises, such nsets, as can be seen nowhere else in these Isles."

It also gave a rare breed of people, equal and receptive to every mood nature. When she turned angrily against them and destroyed all that they ssessed, they, like the patient spider, restored the damage and started all er again. They were a stoic people, resilient to the extreme; bending to :ure but springing back to the task of life which broke many a good .n's bones. They lost a great deal and they gained a great deal, only to e it again. Always they persevered against the odds and became masters the art of creating advantage from disadvantage. Only they could coin : phrase which emerged from the constant drowning of the Fens and the :possession of its beleaguered people: "Nothing is certain but :ertainty."

As I became more involved in this work it seemed entirely appropriate dedicate it to the Fen people of yesteryear, a stoic race if ever there was; :t forgetting their descendants, becoming fewer and fewer with the ars.

Trevor Bevis

# 1. Low Fen Bill Hall

### John Clare of the Fen

IF EVER a true son of the Fens lived it was William Hall ("Low Fe
Bill Hall"), a native of South Kyme, near Heckington, Lincolnshire. He wa
born in 1748 and completed his seventieth year at King's Lynn in 1818.
remarkable character, there is no doubt he had many contemporaries in th
vast Fen region. There were exceptions with Fen Bill. Fortunately for latte
day readers he was well publicised in the elite press of his times, and eve
more remarkable, certain titles were written and published between 18¹
and 1818 by none other than himself. Fen Bill was a kind of poet. Indeed
can be said that he was John Clare of the Fens. He was so filled wi
memories and anecdotes relating to his life as a Fenman, he determined
serialise them. What a pity that the necessary support he deserved was n
forthcoming in greater measure, and thereby, as happens in so mar
instances he took with him to his grave numerous unpublished memories

One is obliged to acknowledge that his literary works were not in h
day considered particularly valuable, and that the gentry were inclined
snigger at the poor writer's efforts. After all, as far as they we
concerned, he was only a Fenman. His hand may have lacked finesse but h
contributions were informatively curious. In our own age, 170 years late
they are seen to be of considerable importance, casting much light upon t
life of Fenmen in the eighteenth and nineteenth centuries. Much of Fen Bil
writing was in poetic style, of personal reminiscences. To those that kne
him they were fairly trivial matter. One set of verses tells how he w
nearly drowned trying to get a plant in the water and was saved by h
mother engaged in washing about thirty feet away. Fen Bill, then only fo
years old, described the event as a miracle, and no doubt it was.

The old-time Fen folk were usually regarded by the elitist upla
inhabitants – their feet firmly secure on dry ground – with unwarrant
disdain; rather lowly aquatic creatures who looked like human beings, the
daily life hinged monotonously to the daily ritual of wildfowling and fishi
and reeping sedge for the great comfort and satisfaction of those th
ridiculed them. But Fen people often turned the laugh against them, for
was the norm for a Fenman and his family (no, they did not have webb
feet!) to live freely off the Fens. They simply unlatched the doors of the
humble abodes, reached out and caught a plump, tasty duck! Our Fen B

most painted such a scene in his "Sketch of Local History," a chain of incidents relating to the state of the Fens in his day:

> Where ducks by scores travers'd the fens,
> Coots, didappers, rails, water hens;
> Combin'd with eggs to charge our pot,
> Two furlongs circle round the spot;
> Fowl, fish, all kinds, the table grac'd,
> All caught within the self same space;
> As time revolv'd, in season fed,
> The surplus found us salt and bread;
> Your humble servant, now your penman,
> Liv'd thus, a simple, full-bred Fenman.

Not so simple our Fen Bill. One almost envies him the abundant larder outside his kitchen door. And what is more, the surplus could be sold to those arrogant uplanders. How easy it was to obtain replenishment for that excellent fresh stocked table. Our intrepid Fenman went on:

> Pray, sirs, consider had you been
> Bred where whole winters nothing seen,
> But naked floods for miles and miles,
> Except a boat the eye beguiles;
> Or coots in clouds by buzzards teaz'd.
> Your ear with seeming thunder seiz'd;
> From rais'd decoy there ducks on flight,
> By tens of thousands darken light.
> None to assist in greatest need,
> Parents but very badly read;
> Were any sent by stress of storm,
> 'Twas much if they could ought perform,
> Scarce five times in the year from home,
> And visitors as seldom come.
> No conversation strike the mind
> But of the lowest, vulgar kind;
> Such scenes attend your ears and eyes,
> For weeks and days, and months, and years.
> Five miles from either church or school,
> No coming there but cross a pool;
> Kept twenty years upon that station,
> Without six months of education;
> Traverse the scene, then weigh it well;
> Say, could you better write or spell?

2

A verbal clout indeed.

The "coots in clouds" that Fen Bill mentions were coots scattered ove
many acres feeding and nesting but if a buzzard approached, in panic, e
masse they were up and away. If a gunner happened to be around when th
happened he could easily kill forty or fifty wildfowl in a single shot. Fe
Bill was keen that his educated critics digest the facts, and even if they ha
been brought up in palacial mansions, there were things they did not know
They could never be a match for the intuition and adriotness of
thoroughbred Fenman.

> *Why such as your parson can't preach on, no doubt;*
> *For here's subjects some persons know nothing about . . .*

At great length he goes on to tell that he was born in a "coy," an
bred in a mill; that he was taught water to grind and to kill ducks. He sa
coots lying flat on their backs, and that he stood upright to row, quite
difficult thing to do, and laid himself flat in a boat covered with a shade
camouflage (or deceive as he says). He took geese, ducks and coots wi
nets stretched over stakes and on a calm day went to catch drakes. That h
gathered as many eggs as he could carry, and cut tracks in the flags whic
was sedge, to decoy the fish to a chosen point where he could lift them. H
saw rudd run by shoals being "dreadully venomed" by rolling in slike.

> *. . . Few parsons, I think, can explain all their meanings,*
> *In theory, I think, they may pretty well do,*
> *But the practical part they have never gone through.*

It seems that Fen Bill and a good many other Fenmen in his tim
suffered the derogatory opinions of local clergymen, most of whom wei
upland natives. The majority could not afford to have their sermon
printed. Perhaps they knew they would not sell them. But Fen Bill publishe
his own work, and spoke out against the arrogance which beset him and t
working classes in the country.

His attempts at poetry give a fair indication of the hardness of fen lif
He mentions that fen farmers had sometimes to use six horses to plough t
difficult soil. In mentioning "coy" he means a decoy where he lived fc
many years. He comes out with odd words and he is probably quoting fc
language. What was a "trammel" for instance? Another Fenman of the nan
of Bailey (descended from the Huguenots) explains that it was a kind
dragnet like a fishing net held aloft by long posts to catch wildfowl at nigh
But I wonder what exactly did Fen Bill mean with "hingles," "hopnets
"slike" and "tannings." And how do coots "clapper claw"; what do they do
for anyway?   These must be old provincialisms which, like the fen as B

was familiar with has long since vanished. Not surprisingly for a man of his observational powers, in a short description of Kyme, he gives an illustration of the neglected state of drainage in the late 18th century. There was a distinct lack of co-ordination among those involved with the undertaking and many farmers took matters into their own hands, erected their own wind engines, and succeeded to pump water from their own fields into a neighbours. It was a time when the engines which looked like windmills except, as Fen Bill wrote, they "grind water," seemed engaged in a losing battle. He quoted an adage that was "in almost every child's mouth in the county":

> *Kyme, God knows*
> *Where no corn grows,*
> *Nothing but a little hay;*
> *And the water comes*
> *And takes it all away.*

It seems that this was the usual reply of Kyme's beleaguered inhabitants when strangers asked them where they came from. But even that discouraging sentiment would change. When the supposedly protective earth banks had been raised higher and a proper system of wind engines and sluices installed run by a single authority, prospects looked decidedly better. The breed of Kyme livestock became famous. So did the coleseed, oats and other mercantile commodities which were produced in the district. So much so, that when a person asked a Kyme inhabitant where he lived, the latter stood himself to full height, expanded his chest and, fixing the inquirer full in the eye, replied:

*"Kyme, sir! Kyme!!"*

Fen Bill gave a page to "The Water Poet's Description of Brothertoft" which was penned by one John Taylor, born about 1580 and died about 1654. He called the place Goostoft and owned most of the land there and kept a large number of geese. "This ancient town," he wrote, "is with watery fens encompassed around. The people have no horse, cow, sheep, ox, ass, pig or sow – no other living thing but geese." Mr. Taylor's remark says a great deal for the Fen economy of the early 17th century. Geese were a valuable asset to a Fenman and if he owned nothing else, no matter. The geese kept him and his family from starvation. They were too valuable to slaughter and feathers from a goose hatched and bred in the damp Fens could be used for all sorts of things. Goose feathers and wool combined well and a Fenman's wealth was measured by these commodities, and also that of cheese.

4

Geese and the goose quill were the hallmarks of a true Fenman and th
man that kept them in quantity was important to his parish.

*And so from place to place he doth aspire,*
*And as his geese grow more he's raised higher;*
*'Tis only geese there that do men prefer,*
*And 'tis a rule - no goose, no officer.*

Low Fen Bill Hall was a man of many parts, with a highly adaptabl
and flexible mind. From one of his publications we learn that not only di
his interest lie with books, he also had a leaning towards mathematic;
instruments. Yet, and more's the pity, "A Biographical Dictionary of th
Living Authors" published in 1816 makes no mention of him. He was boun
to have his critics and he answered them well, and it was regrettable ye
inevitable that the so-called uppercrust viewed him in an unworthy ligh
and therefore without letters to back him up his efforts were deeme
unworthy of their esteemed attention. Really! After all he was only a humb
Fenman with a mere six months' education to his credit! John Clare c
Helpston in Northamptonshire knew all about that attitude. How ridiculou;
These men were gifted by God and they probably achieved more than a
they, which is even more remarkable for scant education in their times.

One of Fen Bill's books, "Reflections Upon Times, Times and Times
or More Than Sixty Years' Tour of the Mind," etc. printed at King's Lyn
in 1816 gives several absorbing accounts of the observations an
experiences of this fascinating Fenman. He tells, for instance, of th
fluctuations in the price of wheat between the first and eighth of October c
one year. "A man showed a sample of wheat on the first; what he asked
cannot tell, but from its handing damp he was told, 'I dare not give yo
thirty shillings for it'; on the eighth the identical sample was asked forty
five shillings per combe and marked off without hesitation. The man wa
even surprised, and said he had lost money for want of asking."

He continued: "Tradition says previous to the year 1750 had been
long succession of dry and favourable seasons, and business kept upon
steady course, insomuch I remember my father giving sixteen shillings pe
quarter for exceeding good high counting barley and his neighbour told hi
he had given 'a longish price.' From that time fluctuations were beyon
belief. The summer of 1756 was very wet. Thunder showers commenced ;
early as March. All Holland Fen lay under water and it was the same a

Floods were disastrous to Fen farmers.
Large numbers of stock perished and the inundated land
could not be used for many months.
Farmers usually made good profits in the dry seasons and
several were described as "very wealthy."
Undeterred by floods, many farmers took to their boats and
sold fish and wildfowl to carriers from London and other
places. The illustration depicts a flooded scene in
1886 and well shows the hazards to farmers
and their livestock.

Crossing the Fens could be a messy and dangerous business.
In some areas church bells were tolled and lamps
hung in belfries at dusk to guide workers and travellers to the
safety of high ground.  On occasions livestock disappeared in
bogs and newly drained fields, and people were lost, too.
Sometimes it was safer, if inconvenient, to make a lengthy
detour rather than risk the shortest and most
difficult route.

*(Picture by kind permission of Cambridgeshire County Council Libraries and Information Service)*

through the Fens to Lincoln. Hay was so mouldy that livestock could not eat it, "neither when it was cut up in fleaks could they chew it till the mould was beat off, and many died . . ."

# FEN WATERSPOUTS

Fen Bill mentioned water spouts which marked wet seasons in the Fens. He had seen as many as six at one time. "My wife and I stood leaning upon our outward gate, looking southward; when a cloud neither enormous nor inconsiderable, passed about parallel to the Dog-and-Doublet from us, but not the least appearance of rain from it. Suddenly a spout hung from it in quite a slanting position and in a very few seconds of time, another sprung from Whittlesey Mere in a slanting position also and met it. We could immediately see the water flow into the cloud with the swiftest rapidity, and as it approached to a perpendicular the more enormous it became.

"On coming to a perpendicular it made a stand for a considerable time, and swelled up to a most prodigious degree, when suddenly it hoisted up a regular sized cloud and we could see the light under it for a quarter of a minute's time. The upper cloud separated from it, only holding by the original spout, and seemed to drag it into its proper region, then dwindled and left its hold."

Going on to resume his account of harvest weather, Hall observed that in 1774 the harvest was marred by heavy rain. During September there was not a fine day, and not a single harvest waggon was used. "Tens of thousands of shoks were fast matted together and literally green," he wrote. The worst season he recollected was in 1799. "I never witnessed a season that caused a more general gloom in the bulk of mankind . . . much corn showed no change to ripen, but kept on the constant grow and swell till it actually grew in the ear." The Fenmen wore very large, strong boots which resisted water. Some actually knelt from boats to get the corn out of the water and convey it to dry land and spread it out to dry.

Fen Bill tells that after his mother had died he had a step-mother described by him as "niggard, crabbed and cross." His wife's name was Juke, and his father's dog called Tyger and that he once had rheumatism in his left arm so severely it throbbed violently, and "without stroke, to touch it, absolutely broke!" This accident disengaged him from his trade as a farrier and cowleech.

He sometimes signed himself Will Wilbeso:

*Kind friends: you who do wish to know the bottom of Will Wilbeso,*
*Now is the time yourselves to treat, For David's age is near*
*    complete.*

6

What Fen Bill is really saying (alluding to David the Psalmist), he ha
almost reached seventy years of age – three score years and ten
Occasionally the enterprising old Fenman waxed apologetic for th
impoverished education during his early and traumatic upbringing.

> *Critics! If you've a mind to throw*
> *Your shafts at old Will Wilbeso;*
> *First send a child to Kyme Low Fen,*
> *Let him stop twenty years and then*
> *Leave him to mere dictates of nature,*
> *Without a mental educator.*
> *Only just leave his battledoor,*
> *Then go to school six months, no more;*
> *Let him be overhead in cumber,*
> *Perplexities too much to number;*
> *Then let him take an author's part,*
> *Try his best typographic art.*
> *Then! if you find he outvies me,*
> *I'll give him leave to criticise me.*

In 1763 there were severe floods in the Lincolnshire Fens; a fine tim
for geese one thinks! But even they were "floated away" and ended up mile
from home. Bill Hall wrote that some of these birds were discovered te
miles away. He was keenly interested in drainage and followed th
achievements of Langley Edwards, engineer to the new River Witham. Bi
credited him with being a very good hand at a battle, and it was a battl
reclaiming drowned land. Our extraordinary Fenman found the time t
record the stories of a few other worthies, one Ashon Goodyer, said to b
one–hundred–and–eight years of age. That venerable gentleman was stewar
of a large estate, but the bursting of certain sea banks ruined the estate an
he took on another large farm but utterly failed. So he came to Wes
Walton, near Wisbech, where his wife managed a little shop and h
employed himself as a cobbler. Later the couple moved to a larger shop a
Tilney and apparently they did quite well.

Fen Bill wrote that in his youth there used to be a Queen of May an
great festivities took place on May Day at South Kyme. If anyone was ill
was the practice to stick a few leeches on them. These small, blood–suckin
worms were plentiful in the Fens and were seen to be very useful i
relieving patients of pressure. ˙ If anyone wanted leeches all one had to d
was find a coot's nest and there would be found thirty or more just waitin
for a customer! A man had only to dip his hand in a fen pool or dyke and
leech would take a fancy to it. No need to pay a doctor who would charg
for the same treatment. Here is another of Fen Bill's quaint "poems":

*I pass Keal Hill at Wainfleet stay*
*And deem it may 'ne plus ultra'.*
*Here halt again and go to sleep,*
*Then ruminate on East Fen Deep,*
*Near where I've seen a mile-long five,*
*Stream, Boston steple, high or higher.*
*Poor fidler, Pinchbeck's case, don't scoff;*
*There both his feet were frozen off.*
*I then coastwise my route pursue,*
*To Fosdyke Wash where at one view,*
*A thousand drowned sheep were seen*
*With scarce a sheep's length space between.*

In frosty weather Fenmen took to ice sledges, and cows took to swimming readily when fodder was scarce. When it came to their doleful way of thinking, pasture was always greener on the other side. Fen Bill mentions "Medley Pie," a Lincolnshire dish produced by dames on the occasion of village feasts. How those feasts did swing! The parish orchestra set feet a'tapping in the streets and in the hall, but the climax came when the Lincolnshire "haggis" was served. It comprised of every meat imaginable and was deliberately "raised" to a great height. Bill knew of an instance where at a feast held at Kyme, a single pie had been sufficient for fifty people. The men of Kyme were called "Fen Coots" while those at Billingay had to suffer being called "Billingay Bogtrotters." This was nothing to do with waste disposal but alluded to work carried out by men in the bogs or marsh.

On occasions Fen Bill lapsed (I think deliberately so as to barb the gentlemen critics into action!). Sometimes he put his thoughts into pure Fen provincialisms, like the following:

*A hammer an' a betle*
*Spalders arr church steple.*

Ah bor, d'ye kip a dicky then? Sheer music to a stranger's ears. Some of Fen Bill's provincialisms were later explained. "Coots clapper-claw lying flat on their backs" – This is assumed to be the attitude of wounded or hard-pressed coots which do throw themselves on their backs and defend themselves with upturned feet. "Crowning of jacks" – the jack is the pike which Fenmen usually caught in a crown net, a kind of hemispherical basket, open at both ends. The "angler" took up his position in a little fen boat and placed his basket down to the bottom of the water. After waiting for a while he then poked his stick into it to discover whether a fish is present.    Evidently enormous quantities of pike were taken in this manner.

8

Fen Bill tells of men "stretched out in boats with a shade to deceive." By this he refers to the use of an artificial cover, camouflage, in the prow of the boat, made up of sedge and weeds so that the prostrate gunner is not easily observed by his intended feathered victims. The gunner propelled the flat-bottomed craft very slowly so as to resemble driftweed. He used short hand-held wooden paddles held beneath the surface so as to leave no tell-tale ripples. What did Bill mean when he wrote "venom'd by rolling in slike?" The Commission of Sewers, 1616-17, refers to "slike" as stagnant water or mud. Nowadays we might refer to it as a form of algae seen frequently in the summer in pools or ditches. In some way it may have benefitted the fish for a similar reason that the hippopotamus likes mud.

We have cause to be grateful to Low Fen Bill Hall - by any means a gifted man - for introducing us in his uniquely quaint manner to the life of Fenmen and their families in an environment best described in his day as oppressive and not without its dangers.

**SUNRISE AT ELY**                    T.B.

# 2.

# Fenland Scene in 1696

A MR. MERRET, Surveyor to the Port of Boston, prepared a Paper for the *Philosophical Transactions* for 1696. Among his observations he writes interestingly about the Fens described by him as pasture grounds feeding a great number of fat oxen and sheep, which were weekly sent to London in droves.

"Our marshes doubtless have been gained from the sea, there being near them . . . such banks and salt hills as Camden mentions at Sutterton. They are fenced chiefly by large dykes, filled with fresh water in the winter and salt in the summer. I have seen the roots of trees that have been dug out of the sands at low water in places near Holbeach and Long Sutton, near a mile from the shore."

Mr. Merret wrote that the fossilised trees were mainly fir and that if one removed a piece of bark it smelled aromatic, something like that of fir-timber in piles that were long submerged in salt water. He continues: "The county people gather up the dung of oxen and cows which they temper with water and spread it on the ground about five inches thick; then cut it into oblong pieces of about a foot, and call them dithes which they use for fuel; in some places they make walls of them for fencing."

One ventures to wonder what effect would transpire if a fire was troublesome and draughts carried the smoke from the dung into the rooms! The author once burned peat purchased from near Swaffham and can vouch that it gave out good heat, especially when it smouldered. A sweet scented aroma filled every room in the bungalow and persisted even when the fire had long been out. The olden time Fen folk also gathered hogs' dung which they saturated with water, stirred it well and strained it, then used it as soap to wash garments. As strange as it may seem it is said that when bleached in summer, the garments became white and sweet, though it is not recorded that the soap dung was used to wash faces and hands!

Camden, writing in the seventeenth century, mentioned an abundance of ruff and reve, wildfowl, the former the cock and the latter the hen, which constantly fought the other. Fenmen had names for fish, the turbot, for instance, he called "brets" and these were caught by employing horses to trail nets on the ground. This indicates that the fish were left on the shore when the tide had ebbed. The Fen people charged their cooking pots with many varieties of food   –   and all for free! Scals, too, were said to be deemed useful in gracing the Fen people's tables, that is those who lived in close proximity to the shore. These were taken by trawl nets dragged by vessels. Supplements for the cooking pot were cod, thornback and plenty of skate which were caught by hooks set out near the shore. So when the Fenman tended his sheep and oxen, or made cheese, he could happily rest assured that his meals for the morrow would be easily retrieved later in the day.

There is no work without hazard. We, living in Fenland are plagued with the usual visitation of midges which near harvest time in their billions assail the delicate senses of human flesh, irritate the eyes, and enter the homes and trap themselves in picture frames. What was God's purpose in inventing the midge! Well, we cannot have it good all the time, can we? Our hard working Fenman of three centuries ago openly cursed the dreaded Fen speciality – the humming gnat. In its season the people of marsh and fen draped themselves with silk nets for protection against insect bites. The "Crowland Sack" was very useful in this way and prevented mosquitoes from sipping the blood of sleepers at night. Naturally in these parts frogs were legion; they were known as Holland waites. Farmers sowed huge quantities of hemp which made outstandingly good rope for use at sea and on land. The female plant was called "femble" and this was true of flax another popular Fenland crop in its day. Flax seed was broken and oil produced as of coleseed introduced by drainage undertakers from Holland.

Salt marsh yielded abundant quantities of "kali geniculacum" which the reader may like to know is samphire, in season purchased on most market places in Fen towns. Very tasty and wholesome to the body it is, too. Olden time Fen farmers attached much value to Carum – a good crop in the pastures; the seed was called "saxifrage" and it found an eager market at London. Very little was found in the Fens and marshes in the way of stone and metal. Sometimes amber was found on the sands and some pieces were quite large. Coal was used to produce coke which in turn dried malt. What was the "Holland bailey?" The Fen people had a saying "Arrested by the Holland bailey" which simply meant one had had the misfortune to be struck down with the Fen ague, a hot and cold shivering sickness, a distressing malady reminiscent of malaria. It was known to severely ravage strangers to the Fens. The natives it seems, suffered it with dignity, and most carried on with their tasks but they were not necessarily immune.

## THE FENS IN 1762

The Fen scene had not appreciatively changed after sixty years. The landscape was dotted with wind engines and additional "cuts" – long straight drains – but still the area was prone to floods in winter. Newly drained fields became so sodden that some farmers, fed up with the seemingly endless flood problems, gave up and went to live on the higher ground. Most stayed, however, and if they did not benefit too much, at least their grandchildren derived the satisfaction of making good profits from places where the yellow-bellied eel formerly lurked in the reed beds and the bream was happy to venom itself in "slike."

Mr. Defoe, a renowned diarist given to touring the country, gave an interesting account of the lowland in 1762. His published work bore the title "A Tour Thro' the Whole Island of Great Britain." He eulogised on the Fens thus:

"As we descended westward we saw the Fen country on our right, almost covered with water like a sea. The Michaelmas rains having been very great that year, sent down vast floods of water from the upland counties; and these Fens being the sink of no less than twelve counties, they are often thus overflowed. The rivers which thus empty themselves into these Fens and carry off the water, are the Cam or Grant, the Great Ouse and Little Ouse, the Nene, the Welland and the river which runs from Bury to Mildenhall . . .

"In these Fens are an abundance of admirable pieces of art called Duckoys (decoys); and it is incredible what quantities of wild-fowl of all sorts - ducks, mallard, teal, widgeon, etc. - they take in them every week during the season. It may indeed be guessed at in some measure by this, that there is a duckoy not far from Ely which yields the landlord 500l a year clear of the charge of maintaining a great number of servants for the management, from whence they assured me at Saint Ives (a town on the Ouse whither the fowls are always brought to be conveyed to London), that they generally send up three thousand couples a week. There are more of these about Peterborough from whence waggon loads are sent up twice a week to London. I have seen these waggons, before the Act of Parliament to regulate carriers, drawn by ten or twelve horses apiece, so heavy were they laden.

"As these Fens appear overwhelmed with water, I observed that they generally, at the latter part of the year, appear also covered with fogs. Glittered with the beams of the sun, the Isle of Ely seemed wrapped up in mist and darkness, and nothing could be discerned but now and then the cupola of Ely minster. One could hardly see this from the hills without concern for the many thousand families confined to these fogs, who had no other breath to draw than what would be mixed with the choking vapours which spread all over the country. But, not withstanding this, the people, especially those that are used to it, live as healthy as those in a clearer air, except now and then an ague, which they make light of, and there are great numbers of very ancient people among them."

Despite the fogs and general dampness of the Fens at the time of drainage operations the natives' constitution encouraged great age.

# 3.

# *Treachery at the decoys*

ARGUABLY THE greatest industry of the ancient Fenland centred on the numerous decoys, small and large, which could be found scattered throughout the length and breadth of the vast level. Long before the introduction of decoys early in the seventeenth century (a method the reader would doubtless consider cruel; but remember it was sound economy to the fen people) there existed a most destructive and reprehensible method of taking wildfowl from the Fens.

It was known as "ducking," a system which severely depleted wildfowl bred in the Fens before the instigation of the more reasonable(?) method of decoying, a method nontheless given to wholesale slaughter. The mediaeval method of ducking involved men in boats, armed with sticks, chasing moulting drakes and flappers that were quite unable to fly into a horse-shoe shaped arrangement of nets, served with pipes or tunnels similar to those of a decoy. It was practised in the Fens until late in the seventeenth century and it was a known fact that many people taking part in ducking were there simply for the sport of the thing. About moulting time, midsummer, several persons, some for sheer pleasure and others purely for profit, took small boats into the reed beds and belaboured the hapless fowl with long poles.

As early as 1534 this method was viewed with abhorrence. The "pernicious practice" of the Fen inhabitants at taking helpless fowl in very great numbers "by certen nettes and other ingyns and polycies" was considered to be quite unnecessary. A system of fines was introduced and for each egg destroyed, stolen, withdrawn or taken from any nest or place of a crane or bustard, the felon was fined twenty pence; for removal of an egg of a bittern, heron or spoonbill (sometimes called a shovelard), the thief was fined eight pence. The Act was practically impossible to enforce and the Fenmen never really recognised it. Eventually it was completely ignored and was not confirmed until 1710 and 1737 when it again proved ineffective.

The Fen economy was served in many ways by the prolific industry of nature, off-shore, on-shore and inland. Of the several means of livelihood available to fen dwellers none were as abundantly successful than the decoys. The natives took as many wildfowl as they needed for replenishing their larders, but the hard cash mainly came from London and other cities. Fowl and fish carted to the upland towns were useful export and boosted the Fen economy, exemplified in the words of Low Fen Bill Hall, "The surplus found us salt and bread." In the eighteenth century most decoys were let for annual rents of between one hundred and five hundred pounds. Daniel Defoe was very interested in this method of taking wildfowl, a destructive if profitable system with the perpetrators who had no thought to the principles of conservation.

The art of working decoys centred on the ability of making nature work for the managers. They bred decoy ducks to lure fellow creatures into nets. The "traitors" were hatched and reared in the decoy ponds and constantly fed by human hand and amply fussed thus establishing the all-important link between man and creature. It also ascertained their determination to stay. However, nature instilled in these hand reared ducks which were perfectly free to wander where they will, to take leave of the pond and decoy men at a certain time of the year. It was this instinctive compulsion to fly away that formed the nucleus of success to profitable decoys. The ducks flew abroad, it is thought to Germany and Holland and, being good ambasssdors they mingled with their own kind and by methods unknown gathered together vast numbers of foreign ducks. One might imagine one saying to foreign friends, "Look here. Come back with us to England and we will show you a superb pond in the Fens with every provision for your needs. Why, there the human kind will actually feed you and you can leave whenever you want to!" Thus beguiled, great numbers of wildfowl were kidnapped from their foreign habitats and led by the treacherous ducks across the sea to the Fens. The unwary fowl followed the decoy ducks as a gundog follows its master. After an absence of several weeks the traitors and vast numbers of foreign ducks, darkening the Fenland sky on their approach, alighted upon the calm, inviting waters of the decoy.

The tame ducks having lured their cousins to the decoy, settled happily in the familiar surroundings were they had received their upbringing and helped the newcomers to merge into the environment. They chatted to them as if telling them that here they should live and that they would fare well. Meanwhile, the decoy man, having observed the birds' arrival, crept around the water's edge, hidden by tall reeds and sedge and quietly threw large handfuls of corn over the top and into the pond shallows where the creatures liked to feed. Along came the tame fowl and hundreds of foreign ducks to receive the food.

This was done for two or three days so as to make the fowl happy and confident. The first feed was thrown in an open, wide area; the second in a similar area; and the third in a narrower place of the decoy where trees hung above the water and the banks and sedge were closer. Finally corn was thrown in the narrowest area where the trees joined overhead like an arbour at a good height above the water. The important thing was to deceive the fowl into feeling free to leave should they want to. A loose net had been spread over the trees, secured by hoops from side to side, and there was a lot of space around for the birds to indulge in their final morsals. All appeared to be quite natural in their eyes and they had no idea as to what was happening.

The decoy man, working behind a specially trained hedge of reeds, went forward and threw corn above the reeds into the channel. The decoy ducks fell upon the corn and invited the strangers to feed upon it, telling them how well English ducks live! By and by all are inside the net which by degrees declines lower and lower, and narrower and narrower, till at the end of the funnel some two hundred yards from the entrance, it came to a point. Imagine hundreds of ducks, including the decoy birds, feeding greedily as they go, the decoy man making certain by his handouts of food that the birds are drawn farther and farther from the entrance and into the funnel so that not a single one will escape.

The final part of the business involved a little dog which had been trained to keep to heel without a sound. At the appropriate time the decoy man gave a signal and the little dog jumped into the water from behind the reeds and with as much splashing as possible swims directly at the ducks, barking all the time. Greatly alarmed, the terrified ducks rose up on the wing and tried to get away, but were prevented from doing so by the arched net in the overhead branches. Falling into the water they were forced to swim along the funnel to the narrower section for fear of the dog behind them.

At the far end of the net another decoy man awaited the ducks' frantic arrival and one by one with great expertise and rapidity he took them out alive with his hands and broke their necks, then threw them onto the ground. What happened to the traitors that had lured the foreign birds into the snare? Some, familiar with the procedure, flew above the pursuing dog and settled upon the pond some distance from the slaughter. Others knowing the decoy man, paddled fearlessly towards him and were taken out like the rest, but instead of being killed, were made a great fuss of and stroked, given a little pond nearby and plentifully fed as reward for their part in the exercise. The dog received a good portion of meat for his services, too.

Old-time wildfowlers employed another effective if destructive method of taking wildfowl in enormous quantities. They used another Fen speciality the punt-gun, a devilish engine with a barrel up to twelve feet long secured to the prow of a flat-bottomed boat. The gunner lay down on the bottom and, peering along the barrel concealed beneath branches and sedge which covered almost the whole of the contraption, stealthily stalked his prey which had settled in dozens on the mere. He propelled the craft slowly and soundlessly with two hand-held paddles beneath the surface so as not to cause the slightest ripple. The floating "island" approached perhaps as many as a hundred or more ducks, then the gunner having got as many birds in his sight as possible, let fly. With a deafening sound the shot spread out in an arc and created pure mayhem. Several Fenmen gained famous reputations in this particular pursuit, including Henry Pickering of Cowbit who lived to the ripe old age of ninety. For sixty years he discharged his mighty gun above the wash between Crowland and Cowbit and had made big hauls. It was his delight, over a mug of beer, to relate how he would creep up to a number of unsuspecting fowl. On one occasion he aimed his muzzle loader with incredible accuracy and bagged as many as twenty-one at a single shot. With another shot he had killed eight wild swans, and in Bourne Fen he carried home in his punt forty-two green plovers in one night! Henry was familiar with the duck decoys and could recall when there were a dozen in Cowbit Wash, yielding in a season no less than five thousand birds for London markets.

Came the spring and the intrepid wildfowler gathered baskets of duck eggs, and by way of a change at other times helped himself to large quantities of tench, eels and pike. These were not always caught by line and hook. A really adept man could place his hand very slowly beneath the fish and gently tickle its belly, working his fingers towards its tail. With a swift movement he gripped the tail and landed the fish beside him. Sometimes a thick string was used to noose the fish as it rested beneath the surface.

# 4.

# *Attempts to protect fowl*

THE FENMEN found in the abundance of water fowl a means of subsistence, not without handsome profits. "Fen Slodgers" took toll of wildlife by every means possible and wild fowling was the chief means of their livelihood. Lapwings, knots and dotterells in about 1512 would fetch 1d. each; seagulls, plovers, woodcocks and red shank 1½d. each; pigeons tern and snipe three for a penny; stints, six for a penny; ruffs, reeves and partridges, 2d. each; and bitterns and curlews, 1½d. each.

Being practically unrestrained by law the Fenmen at appropriate seasons assembled in great force and had their yearly drive of the young ducks before they took wing. Beaters worked a wide track of marsh and the birds would be driven into a net. In this way it was frequently possible for as many as two thousand fowl to be caught in a single session. Fuller writing about Crowland, centuries ago, commented: "Their greater gain is from the fish and the wild ducks that they catch, where are so many that in August they can drive into a single net three thousand ducks. They call these pools their 'cornfields,' for there is no corn grown within five miles."

Sooner or later an Act of Parliament had to be devised to protec hapless wildfowl. During the reign of Henry VIII this came about in these terms: "An Act agenst the Destruccyon of Wilde-fowle at such time as the seid olde fowle be mowted and not replenysshed with fethers to flye, nor the yonge fowle fully feathered perfyctly to flye."

The undrained Fens covered a vast area and this was a difficult if not impossible Act to enforce in its remoter regions; it apparently failed to effect all that was desired. Another Act of Parliament brought out in the reign of Queen Ann made it an offence to take birds at unseasonal times. If a wildfowler killed a bird out of season and was caught, he could expect to be fined five shillings.

Fen dwellers had necessity of natural food supplies and one rightly assumes to a certain extent it was their birthright. Profits made from selling the surplus to markets beyond the Fens introduced the means of enjoying little luxuries manufactured in the uplands. Nothing could better the stout Fen reeds and these were highly desired, not only in the Fens, but in regions beyond. The "Slodger" added to his income by gathering reed which grew abundantly and could make a height of twelve feet. They were

*A view of the Lincolnshire Fens as seen in the nineteenth century from the tower of Crowland Abbey. Surrounding the ancient building, the malarial aspect of oppressive marsh tried the endurance of the normally stoic Fen people.*

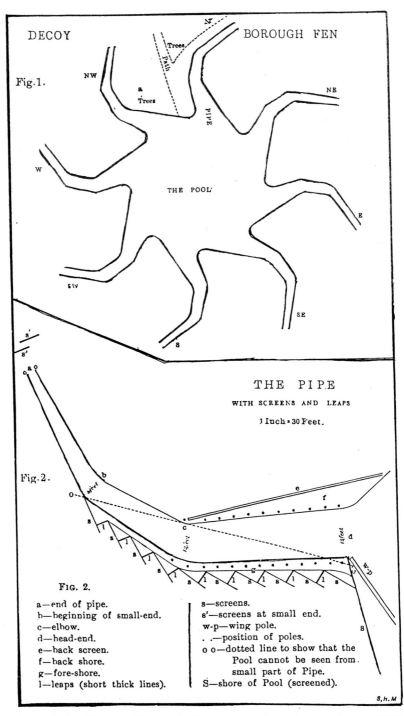

DECOY      BOROUGH FEN

Fig. 1.

N'

Trees

Path

NW

a
Trees

PIPE

NE

W

THE POOL'

E

S W

S E

S

THE PIPE

WITH SCREENS AND LEAPS

1 Inch = 30 Feet.

Fig. 2.

o o

o o

b

e

f

O

c

d

s

FIG. 2.

a—end of pipe.
b—beginning of small-end.
c—elbow.
d—head-end.
e—back screen.
f—back shore.
g—fore-shore.
l—leaps (short thick lines).

s—screens.
s'—screens at small end.
w-p—wing pole.
. .—position of poles.
o o—dotted line to show that the
    Pool cannot be seen from
    small part of Pipe.
S—shore of Pool (screened).

S.H.M

*Plan of the Decoy, Borough Fen, near Peterborough, c. 1890* especially useful for thatching roofs before tiles and slates came into general use. A reed bed was a source of good income, and Camden observed that a stack of reeds harvested carefully was worth £200 to £300. By now readers will begin to appreciate why the Fen people vigorously opposed drainage schemes and that it was certainly not true as some writers in the past inferred, that the Fens comprised a useless watery waste. Fenmen argued against this point in vehement fashion and published their opinions as well as unlawfully resorting to blowing up sluices and deliberately breaching river banks. It did a little good as when drainage was effected some concession came about under the "Lynn Law" which recognised their plight and allowed decoy ponds or meres to be exempt from interference.. This was a hollow compromise, however, as ponds and meres in the Fens existed as long as the rivers and watery lands continued to fill them. The drainage undertakers knew that, as well as the Fenmen, and that one day the water must be carried away to the outfalls and the meres cease to exist.

The demise of the decoys was to affect the Fen economy in disastrous terms. Decoys in the region slowly dried out but a few were persevered with and even devised as late as the nineteenth century. At Ashby in Lincolnshire the decoy was established in 1833-34 and down to 1867 each day's capture was recorded in a very businesslike manner. It amounted to an average take per annum of 2,741 head of wildfowl. The largest number taken at a single drive during late seasons at Ashby was one-hundred-and-thirteen wild ducks, and on the same day two-hundred-and-forty-eight ducks were netted altogether. In thirty-five seasons the total amounted to nearly one-hundred-thousand wildfowl made up thus: wild duck, 48,664; teal, 44,568; wigeon, 2,019; shoveller, 285; pintail, 278; gadwall, 22. Not very inspiring to conservationists but a viable means of livelihood to the Fenmen.

On the coastline, or "flats" on the broad stretches of saline marsh great lengths of netting were erected, six feet high and from one-hundred yards to a quarter-of-a-mile long, suspended between poles. This was an ancient method and the devices were known as "Flightnets" and made of fine wine. The best time to make good catches was wild, moonless nights, known locally as "November darks." Thousands of migrant fowl arrived at that time of the year. As early as possible at ebb tide the wildfowler came to collect the birds snared in the nets before crows and seagulls gathered to seize the victims. Many species tangled together - wigeon, plover, knots, curlew, stints and larks. Heavier birds such as a flock of geese or ducks in flight sometimes broke the nets or caused lengths to collapse. On occasions when the wildfowler arrived he found wild geese in the netting and they, too, were taken. Large birds sold at two shillings apiece and the small, or half birds" at they were called made from sixpence to six shillings a dozen reckoning four as a couple)

How different the vast Fen would have looked, and sounded, three-and-a-half centuries ago, before it had been almost squeezed dry by large numbers of hated engines and intersected by montonously straight artificial waterways. It was written by a Doctor Fuller that the Fens may be termed the aviary of England and that the various birds were known to be delicious wild-fowl, being more dainty than some because of continual motion. Knutes and dotterells were numerous in the Fens, the doctor wrote. According to him the knute is a delicious bird brought out of Denmark at the charge and for the use of King Kanutus (Canute) when he became King of England. "As it has a royal name, so it is esteemed royal dainties and no county (except Lincolnshire) almost hath them but this . . ."

The English Fens never ceased to amaze Camden and he lucidly expressed his appreciation of the lowlands capacity for wildlife: "At certain times of the year, not to mention fish, amazing flights of fowl are found all over this part of the country; not the common ones which are in great esteem in other places, such as teal, quails, woodcocks, pheasants, partridges, etc., but such as have no Latin names, the delicacies of the table and the food of heroes, fit for the palates of the great – puittes, godwittes, knuts, which I take to be Canute's birds, for they are supposed to come hither from Denmark. Dotterell, so-called from their extravagant dotishness, which occasions these imitative birds to be caught by candlelight."

The dotterell acted like a clown and was indeed an expert at imitating human beings! Well, some of the things that human beings can do, anyway. It was an act of folly on the bird's part as, in short, whatever the wild fowler did, the bird did the same. If he held out an arm, the dotterell put out a wing; and if the man held out a leg, so did the bird. Meanwhile the fowler drew near while the dotterell was thinking about the next move, and the net was drawn over it.

Camden was writing about the West Fen of Lincolnshire which "is the place where the ruffs and reeves resort in great numbers, and many other sorts of water fowl which do require the shelter of reeds and rushes, and migrate thither to breed. For this fen is bare, having been imperfectly drained by narrow canals which intersect it for many miles . . . The whimbrels only appear for a fortnight in May, near Spalding, and then quit the country. Opposite Fosdyke Wash during summer, are vast numbers of avosettas, called there 'yelpers' from their cry as they hover over the sportsman's head, like wings. Knuts are taken in nets along the shores near Fosdyke in great numbers during winter, but disappear in spring."

*Bringing in the harvest: West's Farm, near Wisbech, circa 1926*

*This is a typical Fenland scene from the 1920's. Women working on farms was common practice following the tradition of the previous two centuries. The author's mother, brought up on a farm, could handle horses with ease and daily assisted her father in the fields and her mother in domestic chores.*

*Loading a Fen lighter with sugar beet at Nordelph, 1933*

*Barges and lighters made good use of the Fen river system with easy access to numerous towns and villages. There are almost 400 miles of artificial and natural waterways in the Fens, and certain towns, such as March on the old course of the River Nene had their own fleets engaged in the transportation of sugar beet, potatoes, corn, flour, coal and timber, etc. There were eight barges at March in 1580. This mode of commercial transportation continued well into the twentieth century.*

# 5. *Three score geese and a pelt*

GEESE WERE an excellent commodity in the Fens. They could be found all over the area in small and large flocks, but the most numerous flocks were kept near Spalding. In modern times these birds are deemed invaluable as "watch dogs," and can be usually found on Fenland farms. They are quite useful for keeping grass down in large gardens and excell particularly well in this way in churchyards. They do not tolerate strangers as the writer well knows. On one occasion he visited Isleham church, near Soham, and having inspected the building, found to his dismay six of the feathered "dogs" waiting for him at the exit. Wings spread, necks extended and emitting raucous honks the geese completely blocked the pathway and yours truly withdrew into the porch to consider the best way of walking, running or flying(!) to the road a little distance away.

He was well aware that geese are quite capable of damaging the hunam leg with a sharp flap of a wing, even breaking one, if they so desire. In a quandary, he considered making a run for it but thought better. Setting his eyes on distant trees he stepped out cautiously, ever so slowly, as if he had not a care in the world! True to form the flock warned him and formed a half circle around his dithering legs as he stepped very gently towards the lych-gate. Never more than twelve inches from yours truly the geese escorted and chastised the intruder all the way to that blessed gate which sprang to and barred their exist. One breathed again and on the other side the flock hooted and honked, either exasperated that that audacious person had got away or in a frenzied display of victory at seeing him off. Frankly, at that stage I could not have cared less!

Partly for that reason the olden time Fenman could rely on the birds to warn against thieves and predators, and they played not an inconsiderable rôle in the Fen economy. In these parts geese were honoured in at least one proverb: *"The Fenman's dowry is three score geese and a pelt."* Goose feathers were greatly valued in the country, in fact, according to Wheeler the "goose-coat" or feather bed occupied premier place in the ranks of family heirlooms. As the birds were such a profitable investment they were accorded all honour and it might be said that the Fenman thought more of them than he did of his family! So cossetted were the geese, during the breeding season they were taken into the cottages and even occupied the bedrooms, sleeping in comfortable wicker pens placed one over the other.

The geese were attended by the "gozzard" whose duty was to lift the birds off their nests and to water and feed them, then later place them back on their nests. These men were so familiar with every bird that they knew the exact nest peculiar to its feathered occupant. If a goose was returned to the wrong nest the whole community was thrown into confusion and, if the geese could think, the demeanour would be regarded as unforgiveable! In order to increase the output of feathers the geese were plucked five times a year, a painful process accompanied with a great deal of protest. There were special days to do this – Lady Day for quills and feathers; at Midsummer, Lammas, Michaelmas and Martinmas for feathers only. Obviously, quills taken at Lady Day were in prime condition for the craftsman's hands. Live birds produced the best quality feathers, each bird yielding at the rate of threepence per year. At various places in the Fens the geese were "winged" each quarter. On an average each goose yielded ten feathers, these selling at five shillings a thousand. In 1813 a thousand goose quills made 20 shillings. According to records one man kept a flock of one-hundred-and-sixty geese and, in a good season, he reared seven hundred. On average a bad season produced five hundred. They sold at two shillings, the feathers amounting to one shilling and eightpence. To keep the birds was expensive, each averaging two shillings and sixpence which purchased corn. However, a "gooseherd" generally made a net profit of £40.

The highly profitable decoys suffered considerably when marsh and fen was enclosed and drained. Reclaimed tracts rapidly starved decoys of water and dried-out sites eventually turned over to arable use. A few former decoys are still to be seen, relegated to mere ponds enclosed by a few trees and bushes which serve to relieve the flatness of the countryside as well as affording sanctuary to wildlife. As a result of the demise of Fen decoys large numbers of people were made redundant.

In their heyday ten decoys situated in the Lincolnshire Fens kept the London markets supplied on an annual basis with thirty-one thousand two hundred birds, mainly widgeon, duck and teal. This was extraordinarily good as five thousand was considered to be a profitable number. As a side-line the cultivation of the "moss-berry" was deemed useful to the economy but only on a small scale involving a total of three-hundred acres of Lincolnshire fen. It was not a natural Fen product but was introduced to certain low-lying areas at the beginning of the eighteenth century by a person from Westmorland which was renowned for perfect moss-berries. The average yield in the Fens amounted to two thousand pecks a season but occasionally four thousand pecks were harvested, pickers earning on average five shillings a week. Markets for this commodity were in Lancashire, Cambridgeshire and Yorkshire, the latter mentioned producing excellent cranberry tarts. When drainage had been effected few moss berries were collected.

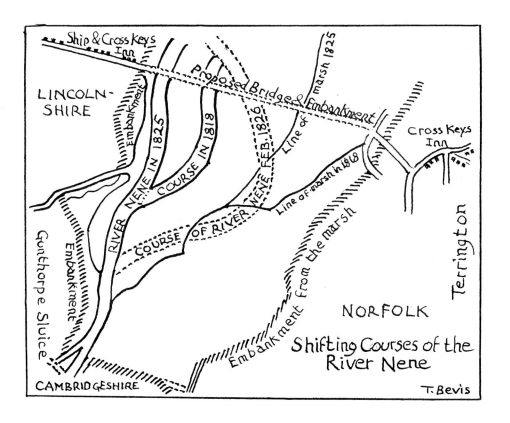

Plan of the bridge and embankment at Sutton Wash, based upon
W. Watson's "An Historical Account of the Ancient Town and Port of
Wisbech" (1827). The plan shows the channel of the River Nene which
was notorious for its tendency to shift. Shifting water courses were
common in pre-drainage times. They were a considerable
problem to Fen people, some channels known to alter course
overnight and endanger lives and property. Enterprising Romans built
miles of embankments to protect marshland areas from the sea.
When in circa 400 the Romans were recalled to protect their homeland,
the great embankments were unmaintained and the sea breached them
in numerous places, causing outfalls to silt, and rivers
overflowed the great level. The Fens remained mostly under water from
the fifth century and were adjudged entirely drained in the latter half of
the nineteenth century.

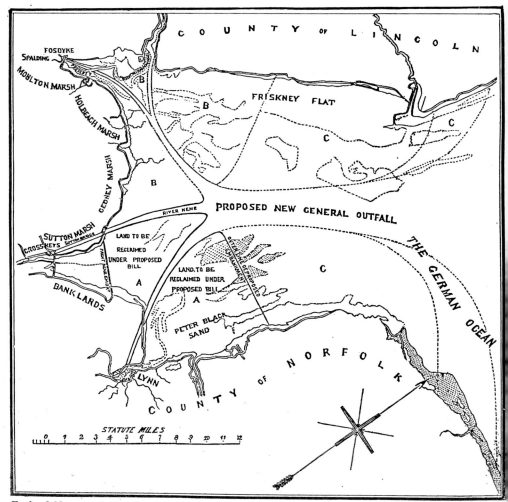

Fenland Notes and Queries, April 1906

*Reclamation of the Wash has long been considered a possibility. A major scheme (above) was proposed in 1839. If it had materialised it would have changed almost the entire bay from sea and sand flats into virile agricultural grounds. Feasibility of converting the Wash into productive land and fresh water reservoirs was studied well into the twentieth century.*

# 6.
# *Hard labour for the Fenmen*

NOTHING WAS more trying to Fenmen than the environment. Those that lived nearest the sea – an area more aptly defined as Marshland – had the worst of the deal. They certainly had more problems than did their cousins living reasonably secure on the islands which varied from a few feet to as high as eighty feet. Not only did the men of the marsh have to wrestle with swollen rivers carrying water from distant upland regions, they grappled helplessly with a far more insidious enemy – the sea.

Anyone that loves old churches recognises the Fens as the home of some of the finest fanes in the country. Those within a stone's throw of the sea are without doubt exceptional by any standard, and the logical mind readily comes to the conclusion that mediaeval Fenmen were not short of a shilling or two. Even if the sea did breach the Roman embankments as it did on countless occasions, fairly rapid recovery seemed to take place and the Fenmen girded up their loins, rebuilt their stock and their cottages, repaired the churches and got on with the job. Several of the old sea banks form roads elevated above the silt fields and overlook a vast area even more devoid of trees than the inland Fens. A sea bank was called "vallum" (wall), the term surviving in some of the villages in close proximity to the ancient earthen barriers, viz. Wal(soken), Wal(ton). and Wal(pole).

## OVERTHROWN BY THE SEA

Few churches situated in a wide arc sweeping from north of Boston and following the Wash coastline to King's Lynn, escaped repetitional washings from the sea. These fanes, some aptly described as "queens" and "kings" and written of as "cathedrals in miniature," represent the great building styles from Norman to the Perpendicular periods. Their foundations are reinforced by wooden rafts and considering the very nature of the soil and the amounts of salt and fresh water by which they were subjected over the centuries, it is indeed a miracle that any survive. A few accounts of those dreadful inundations were recorded on documents and can be seen in a few churches with commemorative plaques. One such plaque at West Walton tells of those times in the seventeenth century when weaknesses in the earthen barriers caused breaches for the water to exploit which resulted "in all Marshland being overthrown by the sea."

22

At Terrington St. Clement the massive mediaeval tower, detached from the pinnacled church by a mere twelve inches, afforded sanctuary on more than a few occasions to the inhabitants who had abandoned their homes to the fury of the sea. There they waited for boats from King's Lynn to bring them provisions usually collected by the burgesses of the Norfolk borough. Neighbouring Terrington St. John's, too, suffered from sea incursions, being occasionally isolated from its neighbours by inundation. The church has a priest's house of three storeys erected between the slender tower and the church aisle, and in these uncomfortable, cold and damp confines the cleric waited for the water to recede or the arrival of a boat to carry him away to a safer place. The old church of St. John the Baptist at Parson's Drove entirely lost its chancel in the seventeenth century when water swept into the village through breached embankments a few miles away. The "temporary" east wall of the nave still remains.

There are accounts of hamlets being utterly destroyed by ravaging floods. Dolpoon, thought to have been situated in the region of Sutton Bridge was utterly erased from the map.

*"When Dolpoon stood*
*Long Sutton was a wood."*

This disaster helped Long Sutton to develop into a prosperous little market town surrounded by rich silt land. Near Newton, in a place named Saltmarsh, once stood a church or chapel devastated by storms of the sea. It was abandoned and the people transferred to a place more remote from inundation. This was probably Newton. Strange tales were recorded of Saltmarsh and its little chapel "and bodies anciently buried there in which chapel wondrous *(nonnullorum miraculorum genera)* and shining lights had appeared of old and still appeared at night." A hermitage existed near Parson's Drove in olden times, this observed as early as 1107 and a map of Wisbech Hundred (c. 1540) depicts a chapel standing on the site which was known as Endewicke ("the dairy farm by the ford through the Eau") and which was probably, like several other Fen settlements, wiped off the face of the earth by the action of the sea. So severe were these disasters it was written that during the sixteenth century a ship was driven ashore by fierce gales which forced the sea many miles inland. The vessel came to rest on the roof of a house and the sailors, hearing the terrified cries of a woman in a room beneath, saved her and her unborn child from a watery grave but were unable to rescue her husband.

The suffering of Fen people in pre-drainage and post-drainage eras is undescribable. Always equal to the occasion, they turned their faces to the storms, and in most appalling conditions repaired the breached embankments, rebuilt farms and livestock, then in defiance of nature did

23

"unthinkable" things which many lesser mortals on the uplands, shaking their heads in disbelief, declared would invoke the wrath of God. The Fenmen erected new embankments against the sea and excluded it from large areas of its former domain. Slowly the sea was pushed back and the task of reclaiming drowned land continued in defiance of tides, gales and storms. Cast an eye over the siltland today! Where fine crops are gathered little remains to remind onlookers and workers of that bitter struggle between men and nature. The colour of the soil gives the best clue. On the horizon an embankment carrying vehicles marks the site of the boundary of the saltmarsh and the briny beyond. Look around and here and there will be seen elegant church towers which witnessed it all, their lower stages immersed in water for months at a time.

Sea banks were built during the Roman and mediaeval eras on the farthest edge of useable land supporting cattle and sheep. Standing upon the existing sea banks one will gain a good idea what the medieval Fen farmer saw. Against the bank a considerable amount of flotsam and jetsam has gathered in a long, snaking corridor on which wary feet can tread. It is always risky to proceed along the seaward side and only those familiar with the marshes and creeks and not averse to generous amounts of mud are advised to explore, armed with the cautionary advice of a tide timetable. It is a different world, a lonely world, a world of abundant sounds and aromas of nature. It is satisfyingly free for eyes and mind to roam. Here are the wide horizons – the world of the embattled Fenmen.

Through constant natural process the saltmarsh received layers of silt and it was gradually enclosed, not by hedgerows as in the inner areas, but by earth baulks. Over a decade the saltmarsh converted to freshmarsh and upon it grew coarse grass. It was then ready to amalgamate it with parish lands. The old sea bank became a decaying baulk and a new bank erected nearest the sea. The men of the Fens were very efficient at this hard, dangerous and repetitional task. Perusing old maps indicate all along the shores of the Wash sea-barriers were continually being erected and breaches repaired and the sea, despite its habitually ferocious nature did, in fact, lose ground. A few centuries ago this activity probably contributed to severe silting of natural water courses creating problems to natural drainage in places inland. Some rivers were known to change course in a period of a few days and even overnight with sometimes disastrous consequences. The saltmarsh accumulated more rapidly on the southern shores of the Wash which tends to receive clay and other deposits from the Yorkshire coast. Reclaimed marsh was much less in the northern area. In the reign of James the First, Surfleet in the north, held about two-hundred-and-fifty acres of marsh beyond the sea-bank, and at Leake a mere thirty acres were added over a course of many years. But at Moulton and Gedney in the south 1,554 and 2,000 acres of reclaimed land respectively were held.

Low marsh lay in the area where the sea had retreated. As the marsh slowly dried out, it began producing crab grass, cotton lavender and samphire. Soon there was a profusion of coarse grass. This marsh was worth 1d. an acre compared with high marsh valued at 2d. an acre. The lower price did not necessarily reflect the quality of grass but took into account risk of flooding. Generally the marsh appeared indistinguishable, "high" and "low" occupying the same level. Fen people recognised the qualities of grass, and the areas of reclamation were divided by ditches and embankments.

Each generation became familiar with changes in the soil quality and the parish boundaries were constantly expanding as more marsh was reclaimed. This constant expansion was not always attributable to man's design. In one instance early in the seventeenth century farmers and fishermen near Boston increased their saltmarsh through a variation in the water channel's course. The wind, they said, had forced a new course through the marsh to an area a mile nearer the sea. Such changes in creek and river channels were not uncommon. It reflects a similar occurance when the River Ouse which had its tributary near Wisbech, rapidly diminished and became badly silted as the Ouse, with men's help, followed a more direct course between Littleport and King's Lynn.

During the 1570's many such changes occurred in the Fens. Creeks and inlets which afforded passage for small fishing vessels, began to silt badly and became unnavigable. Old folk at Frampton, Lincolnshire, recalled the times forty years previously when ships sailed up the creek there and discharged cargo within "two shutts" of the old sea-bank. At the time that this observation was made vessels could no longer approach within a mile of the bank. John Orden, a resident of Holbeach, had said that he had heard of a creek which stretched from the sea to the sea bank at Whaplode and "the wives of fishermen could stand thereupon and call their husbands home to dinner." How convenient that was!

# EXCELLENT PASTURE FOR SHEEP AND HORSES

Fish, naturally, were plentiful in the marsh creeks and in the freshwater meres and rivers inland, as well as an abundance of wildfowl which graced the tables of Fen folk. Oxen bred in the Fens and marsh were regularly supplied to the Navy. In 1513-14 the navy victualler purchased two-hundred-and-fifty-three fat winter-fed oxen (slaughtered and salted at Saltfleet). He also purchased three-hundred-and-twenty-two oxen at Wisbech and one-hundred-and-sixty-four at Stamford and Peterborough reared on the water meadows at those towns. In the marsh proper, new and old grazing pasture lay to the rear of the sea-wall. It was tolerably good for fattening cattle, but more especially so it excelled in grazing for horses. Sheep fared excellently too, on these pastures and produced heavy fleece, but wool from the Fens was generally cheaper than that from the Cotswolds which rated best. Former marsh when first turned by the plough was so fertile that corn was gathered year after year without so much as an additional farrow. In some Fen areas, particularly near Chatteris, women and children were employed to trample upon young shoots to delay growth.

Land reclamation in the Wash vicinity is a complex story. It tried men to the limit – and in physical and financial terms broke a good many. The title of land gave clues emphasising the sacrifice and reward attending the task. An illustration of this is seen in a survey of Long Sutton carried out in 1609. Village lands within or near this parish received no less than eleven categories. "Free increase land" is self explanatory. "Free burgage land" was that given to tenants for the site of the village. "Dearbought land" was subject to frequent flooding and cost the reclaimers dearly; sometimes it was abandoned and left for fishing and wildfowling. "Workland" was that which tenants were obliged to plough, sow and reap for the owner, usually the lord of the manor. "Conquest land," so-called because it was "won and gotten by labour and industry from the water which did overflow it." A most appropraite definition of the nature of work demanded of the Fen people. Some tenants were under the obligation to stack corn and hay; land thus used was known as "golving land."

Seldom did the men living in the vicinity of the coast find a dwelling place secure from flooding by river and sea. Those inhabiting islands were usually safe from water encroachment, but offshore "harbours" or "cotes" – very low islets of small acreage used for harbouring cattle – were sometimes flooded by excessive amounts of fresh water with disastrous consequences for livestock and owners. All too often weather patterns dictated the difference between poverty and riches for the men of marsh and fen. The same elements, however, imbued the population with a hardness as well as fortitude and courage. It gave Fenmen a rare constitution and well they had need of it. Upland people identified the Fenmen as "cantankerous," a characteristic term linked to the hard qualities and demands made upon them. Few, however, gave up the hard labour. The islands, marsh and fen were put to good use and an excellent inland communication between the parishes was maintained via the numerous waterways, causeways and meres. In this respect local rivers far exceeded the lanes and roads on the upland which were sometimes impassable during winter and very expensive to maintain. The Fen farmers, fishermen and wildfowlers were a unique breed of people and the part they played in maintaining the Fen region, thereby stimulating the local economy, evokes unstinted admiration. It was a way of life which worked well for the communities and the fact that Fenmen hindered the drainage schemes by fair means and foul is understandable.

# BURN THE SOIL AND MAKE CROPS GROW

The main bone of contention with Fenmen was the threat to their livelihood from draining schemes. And worse still, among the perpetrators were foreigners led by Sir Cornelius Vermuyden, a skilled Dutch land drainage engineer. This man successfully encouraged large numbers of foreign people to settle in the Fens, including Huguenots and Walloons from France and the low lying areas of Belgium and Holland. Families tore up their roots from their native soil and fled to England to escape religious persecution. After attempting to settle down in various parts of the country these families, despite hostility from the natives, eventually found a haven in the Fens. The principle colony was at Thorney and several lived and worked elsewhere in the area, notably at Parson's Drove, French Drove and Guyhirn. They played an important rôle in the drainage schemes of the seventeenth century and soon adapted to farming the land they had helped to reclaim.

It seemed to the Fenmen that everywhere they turned foreigners stood in the way. Hundreds of Dutch and Scottish prisoners of war were drafted to the Fens to dig drains and improve existing rivers – something the Fenmen would not do. Not surprisingly, ideas to improve the land were usually products of foreign conception, such as the paring plough and burning the top layer of the soil. This was an important operation with Fen farmers, an innovation which beget the more recent practice of burning stubble, now forbidden by law. Peat land scarcely bore the weight of horses in the spring and breast ploughing was introduced. The plough was simply a pole about nine feet long with two pieces of wood, one each side, about thirty inches long at the bottom which was reinforced with iron, turned up at the right side to cut the side of the furrow. The ploughman was clad in a padded apron of sack cloth, or similar, with two slats of wood placed vertically on each side against which rested the long cross handle of the plough. The man pushed it forward slightly under the roots of the herbage, about one or two inches deep, and every two feet or so turned it over with a sudden jerk. The thin furrows after lying a few days were raked together in heaps and then set on fire. This action destroyed the rank vegetation as well as the larvae of pests, and the ashes spread out over the soil, gave it certain virility.

This was done in preparation for a crop of rape or cole, which was extensively grown in the Fens for sheep feed and crushing purposes. Oil from the cole seed was used to steep wool to soften it and also to burn in oil lamps. It was crushed in no less than seven local mills and it was written that one thousand tons of oil was dispatched in ships from Wisbech port on an annual basis. There was an oil mill at Thorney. According to a valuation of about 1653 "for hassocking and burning the hassocks, paring and burning of the sward and sowing with coleseed," the cost amounted to twenty shillings per acre. This popular method was still employed in 1868 and worked out at a cost of twenty-four shillings per acre. The method was commonly employed among French farmers from at least 1600. Burning stubble derived from this practice and it was only in recent years that this was allowed subject to suitable conditions and finally made illegal.

*Gathering sedge near Ely. This nineteenth century engraving may depict Wicken Fen, an admirable example of conservation of fen unchanged for hundreds of years.*

# *So many washings . . .*

**7.**

AT CERTAIN times of the year the men of marsh and fen steeled themselves against eventualities . . . flooding from the sea which, in turn, held back fresh water along the rivers and caused embankments to burst with disheartening consequences. In 1611 an unusual inflow occurred at Whaplode and Holbeach. Very rapidly the incoming tide overflowed saltmarsh to a depth of almost three feet and immediately reclaimed fertile ground was at risk. Creeks tended to change course and that affected parish boundaries. In 1607 Gedney jurors recorded "the numbringe of acres is a verie uncertain thing for us to doe, for there will be some tymes a hundredth acres of marsh ground and within three howers space the best of it will be overflowed with the sea about six foote deep." It was on those occasions when men, beast and buildings were in imminent danger of being "washed" that the inhabitants resorted to boats and found security within church towers.

Embanking and enclosing thousands of acres rightly or wrongly has been seen by many as blatantly interferring with nature. It was proved time and time again that men can never successfully dictate to nature, however noble the cause. Controlled perhaps, but nature bides her time and strikes with awful majesty and strength, leaving the beholder helpless. It happened in ages past and despite all men's efforts with machines and technology, it can happen still. Even in recent times Wisbech was re-visited by a huge surge of tidal water which spilled over the river banks and claimed a life as well as ruining and damaging property. That occasion was a small taste of the dreadful floods occurring in these parts centuries ago which resulted in the loss of hundreds of lives.

The earliest recorded flood in 1236 saturated Wisbech and all but destroyed the Norman castle. Holinshed wrote: "On the morrow after the Feast of Saint Martin and certain days after, the sea burst out with such tides and tempests of wind that the marsh countries near to the sea were drowned and overflown, besides great herds and flocks of cattle that perished. The sea rose continually, inflowing for the space of two days and one night without ebbing by reason of the mighty violence of contrary winds. At Wisbech also and in the villages thereabouts the people were drowned in great numbers, so that in one village there were one hundred corpses in one day."

To this Matthew of Paris added: "The sea was raised much higher than usual and the storm continued for eight days, so that of men, small ships and cattle, great multitudes perished." The vicar of Saint Peter and Saint Paul church, Wisbech wrote of his observations after a flood in 1613 when almost the whole of Wisbech Hundred lay beneath water. This, too, claimed human lives. Sea banks were broken and the loss of corn crops and cattle incalculable. The clergyman wrote: "To the immortal praise of God Almighty that saveth His people in all adversities. Be it kept in perpetual memory that on the Feast of All Saints being the first of November 1613, late in the night the sea broke in through the violence of a north-east wind meeting with the tide and overflowed all Marshland with this town of Wisbech, both on the north and the south, and almost the whole Hundred round about to the great danger of men's lives and the loss of some. Besides the exceeding great loss which these countries sustained through the breach of banks and spoil of corn, cattle and houses which could not be estimated.

"The following year of Our Lord 1614, upon the twenty-third day of March the country was again overflown with the fresh waters which came down in such abundance through the extraordinary great snow that fell in January and February, that only this town whereof the south side was lost, but the greater part of the grounds within the South Eau bank in Holland from Spalding to Tydd Saint Giles was drowned and almost wholly for that year.

*A flooded scene during the inundation of 1862. During times of flood, farmers resorted to fishing and wildfowling.*

"Moreover, a great part of Marshland from the bank called The Edge between the towns and the Smeeth to the new Podike was lost through divers breaches between Salters Lode and Downham Bridge. In conclusion, many towns in Norfolk confining with Marshland and most part of the Isle of Ely" (were drowned).

Of the inundation of 1571, Holinshed enlarged upon the villages and towns affected. He indicated that the water, several feet deep, spread rapidly over vast distances, an awesome phenomenon seen with great clarity in the devastating floods in America in 1993 when the Mississippi and Missouri rivers breached their banks in numerous places. "The sea broke in between Wisbech and Walsoken and at the Cross Keys, drowning Tilney and Old Lynn, St. Marie (Wisbech), Tydd St. Mary, Tydd St. John, Walpole, Walton, Walsoken, Emneth, Jarmans and Stow Bridge, all being in the space of ten miles. These towns and villages were overflowed, that is to say Wisbech, Guyhirn, Parson Drove and Hobhouse" (Hobbs Lot). The chronicler added that one church in the fen was wholly overthrown except the steeple. This might well be at Marshland St. James, where the church nave does not exist and the tower is some distance from the chancel.

At West Walton the outstanding thirteenth century church, foundations of which had been severely affected by repetitional flooding throughout the centuries and which were strengthened in more recent times, displays a tablet perpetuating the harsh times of marshmen and their families:

*"Surely our sins were tinctured in grain;*
*May we not say the labour was in vain.*
*So many washings - still the blots remain."*

Many of the "washings" are doubtlessly unrecorded, yet they are part of the Fenland story - tragedy and an inspiration of the Fen people's stoicness, their ability to bear difficulty and discomfort without complaint. The fact that notable flooding occurred near the coastline does not detract from the bitter experiences of Fen people living inland on and around the islands. Loss of life, livestock and possessions is all the same be it salt water or fresh.

Fendyke Bank from Clough's Cross near Parson Drove formed a very significant barrier against water encroachment. The ancient embankment still survives and as is common to parts nearest the coast the barrier carries a circuitous road. Similar to the Roman sea-bank near Leverington, it was supposed to protect the north side of Wisbech as well as the Tydds, Leverington, Newton, Guyhirn and Wisbech St. Mary. The purpose of Fendyke Bank was to prevent fresh water from upland areas in the vicinity of Bourne from inundating these places. Minor floods could be controlled but once in a while nature really pulled out all the stops.

Water from the direction of Thorney seriously affected 13,400 acres of land in 1437 through the default of one Thomas Flower who worked twenty-four acres in Wisbech High Fen. Apparently he neglected to close a sluice. Other breaches occurred in 1570 and 1770. The water forced a gap in the bank of Abel's Gull where the road is shaped like a horseshoe, the protrusion taking that form when the bank was repaired around the breach. The breach resulted in practically the whole of the land on the east side being unundated to a depth of six feet with disastrous consequences to Wisbech St. Mary, Leverington, Murrow and Parson Drove. It was impossible to grow anything for three years. Floods could occur without any warning and on one occasion people living in the fen near a breached bank fled for their lives to Thorney where they sought refuge on higher, drier ground.

Three and four centuries ago meadowland was more plentiful in the wet fens than now. In the winter there was a tendency for land on the edge of islands to be submerged but during the spring and summer when the water had drained lush grass grew and it was particularly beneficial to grazing herds and flocks of sheep. Some lowly situated parishes were literally in the marsh and perilously near rivers. At Fosdyke in Lincolnshire and at the Wiggenhalls, Norfolk, floods were accepted as a way of life.

Elevated gravel ridges were not too seriously affected by flooding and the Fen islands proper, i.e., March, Manea and Chatteris were practically surrounded with water in winter. The inhabitants took full advantage of the fisheries at all times of the year and turned stock onto water meadows when safe to do so. Islets in the fen barely a few feet above the marsh were put to good use during summer as "harbours" and "cotes."

Despite the hazardous circumstances, working the marsh and fen prior to major drainage schemes was by no means a wasted effort. The watery Fens played an important part in the national economy but change can never be thwarted. The new order of things had to come. Far-sighted capitalists rejoicing in the title of Gentlemen Adventurers (really drainage undertakers) in agricultural terms rightly visualised the potential wealth of the great level. With vigorous protests punctuated by violent action, the Fen inhabitants strived to preserve what they argued was their natural birthright to take fish and wildfowl. Vision and capital won the day.

Even the Fens' greatest son, Oliver Cromwell, who at first objected to any interference with the Fen people's way of life (probably because King Charles would immensely benefit from a successful drainage scheme), came to extoll the area in glowing terms and gave his backing to the work. He would, he said, not only make the Fens a place fit for God to live in, he supported the plan to effectively transform the Fens from a watery morass to a level of prime agricultural importance which would bring about national benefit from achievement quite unparallelled in human endeavour.

# 8. Eking a living from marsh and fen

MARSH and fen are different, but to visitors they are much of a muchness; a vast level with great acreages for most part void of trees and hedgerows, with thousands of miniature islets as it were, divided by a complex arrangement of rivers, drains and dykes. The difference is in the soil, the marsh land a sandy coloured silt the result of centuries of sea action persisting inland from the coast to an extent of about fifteen miles. In the fen proper the soil is comprised of varying shades of brown, the lightest colours a mixture of silt and peat, the darkest shades progressing to near black, a fossilized mixture of decaying leaves and parts of trees and bushes, reed and sedge which year after year fell into the water and decayed to form, hundreds of years later, thick layers of ultra rich soil. It rolls on and on beneath the ample sky to the distant upland, broken here and there by large and small "islands" formed of clay and ordinary topsoil on which developed hamlets, villages and towns.

Fishing and wildfowling – regarded as local birthrights – were the prime occupations of most old time Fenmen, particularly those living near the fringe areas where the lowland meets the highland, facilitating ready access to merchants from principal towns and cities. In addition, extensive husbandry was carried out on the islands. Crops of corn and barley and rearing cattle and sheep demanded a considerable amount of workers' time. The humble eel was a particularly strong asset to the medieval Fen economy, and formed a basis of rent in whole or in part to bishops, abbots and priors holding extensive tracts of fen in the parishes.

After the Dissolution of the monasteries a typical farmer in the year 1560 could be expected to possess a couple of horses, eight dairy cattle, three geese and a pig. His neighbour might vary slightly and additionally keep poultry, a breeding mare, three swine and four dairy cattle. Most farmers had a boat and fishing gear.

In 1690 the scene had not changed a great deal. According to an observer writing in that year . . . "As for wildfowl, about midsummer at moulting time, several persons go in small boats among the reeds and knock the birds down with long poles, being then unable to swim or fly. As for fish there are great quantities, especially pike. The water is deep in some places eight, nine or ten feet. There are also large numbers of geese which live on the grass but taste both rank and muddy, but when fed with corn are as good as others. They make amends in the vast quantity of feathers and quills they provide. The owners pluck them four, five and sometimes six times a year for their feathers, and thrice for their quills. Some persons have a thousand (geese) and more.

"The country people gather up the dung of oxen and cows which they temper with water and spread on the ground five inches thick; then they cut it out in oblong pieces of a about a foot and call them dithes which they use for fuel. In some places they make walls of them for fencing. They also gather up hogs dung and steep it in water, and having well stirred it and so use it to wash clothes which they bleach in the summer, will become white and sweet. As for insects, gnats and midges are in some places very troublesome. Frogs are numerous, called Holland wastes."

People living in London and other large towns and cities recognised the Fens as an abundant source of fish and fowl. Some owners of fen, especially in South Lincolnshire, sent large tonnages of meat and dairy produce to the metropolis. Reed grown in the Fens was well favoured over an extensive area of highland for building purposes. All this enabled the Fenmen to accumulate good profits, but he visualised not without justification that his way of life would be adversely affected if the much trumpeted plans to drain the Fens became reality. Their living would diminish and even disappear if weighted propaganda from the hated drainage undertakers influenced exalted people that could authorise such an adventure. The Fenmen got their heads together and countered the opposing side with their own reasons for leaving the Fens alone.

Small areas of fen had been drained, none too successfully, since the beginning of the sixteenth century. Enterprising bishops and wealthy individuals had already attempted to rid small areas of water two hundred years previously. Early wind engines had been employed in experiments on fen land between March and Elm, but although difficulties had been encountered sufficient progress was made by the perpetrators of these early experiments with their despised "whirligigs" to raise justified anxiety in Fenmen's minds as to their future existence. They responded with their own publication "The Anti-Projector" in the mid 1640's – a reply to the drainage undertakers – "who alwaies vilified the Fens and have misinformed many Parliament men that all the Fens is a meer quagmire, and that it is a level hurtfully surrounded and of little or no value: but those which live in the Fens, and are neighbours to it, know the contrary . . ."

The Anti-Projector gave a good idea as to how valuable the undrained Fens were and that, in addition to large numbers of fish and wildfowl, an infinite number of horses, mares and colts not merely to till the land were valuable to farmers and others on higher ground. Cattle were numerous too, and large dairies could be found in the Fens, furnishing the navy with plentiful supplies of butter and cheese. There were multitudes of heifers as well as Scottish and Irish cattle fattened on fen grazing grounds, and these, in addition to meat, provided hide and tallow.

The Anti-Projector went on to emphasise that the undrained Fens provided fodder which was fed to cows in winter and in turn the animals provided great quantities of compost to enrich the pastures and corn lands "half-in-half, whereby by sea we do, and can (if our navigable rivers be not made unserviceable by the Undertakers pernicious new ditches) abundantly furnish London and the northern parts in their necessities. All which fore-recited commodities make our Fens far more profitable to the owners, lying as they are for grass, than if they were sown with corn, rape or coleseed."

Great flocks of sheep were kept in the Fens and much in the way of hay and course grass which grew well in all weather and provided upland farms and farms in the remotest of places with sufficient fodder for cattle when, in some years drought and severe winter conditions severely depleted normal supplies of feeding stuffs. That was never the case in the Fens which supplied prodigious amounts of osier, reed and sedge to upland farmers and these commodities set large numbers of poor people on work.

The leaflet insisted that should the Undertakers seize as much as one-third of the Fens, many thousands of cottagers "would go a-begging." Not only would the corn grounds and pastures be destroyed but also the poor and people would be unable to help them. "What is coleseed and rape?" asked the Anti-Projector in derisive tones. "They are but Dutch commodities and but trash and trumpetry and pills land, in respect of the fore-recited commodities (those grown in the Fens) which are the rich oare of the Commonwealth."

This propaganda was vouchd for fifty years later in 1696 by Christopher Merret, surveyor, who unbiasedly wrote that he had observed the abundance of fish and fowl and that the Fens abounded no less with quadrupeds "as beasts, sheep especially – which will grow fat – and horses." The drainage undertakers were quick to point out a tract of fen between Spalding and Crowland, which they regarded as a showpiece underlining what their reclamation plans would achieve. On it grew "very great crops of oats and also large quantities of Rapsum Sylv (coleseed) whereof they make oil."

# FEN ECONOMY UNCHANGED

There had been little or no change in the Fen economy for a hundred years. Nature dictated the pace and little if any difference had been noticed in production. It was much the same in 1598. If a Fenman kept several cattle he was deemed as being wealthy.    In upland counties the average number of cattle on a farm between 1500 and 1530 was six; in the Fens it was ten, the largest herd about forty. A man with between five and seventeen animals was of average fortune. A wealthy Fen farmer's household had a dairy with milk vessels, a cheese press and vats. A man of substance like John Hood of Sutterton, at his death in 1537 left ten stones of cheese and two stones of butter which was four times the average farmer's fortune. Another Fen farmer did even better with fifteen stones of cheese and five stones of butter produced by his herd of twenty-two cows. A less wealthy farmer like Henry Wythington of Tydd St. Mary in 1537 had property valued at £4 10s. 4d. (all debts paid), and just ten stones of cheese in his house.

Horses reared in the Fens were usually sold to neighbouring regions. In Leicestershire in the 1530's ploughing was mainly carried out by oxen. Arable land in the Fens was not sufficient to work the usual number of half-a-dozen horses and while large numbers of horses were certainly bred in the Fens during the sixteenth century they were reared for military purposes and sold to private owners.

Sheep played a significant part in the Fen economy. Sizeable flocks could be seen grazing the island commons and in early summer when certain low grounds emerged from winter inundation, flocks were let loose on fresh grazings. The finest wool produced in South Holland Fens of Lincolnshire was rated a fractionally better price than could be obtained in Norfolk. In 1536 wool made 4s. 8d. a tod but the finest wool came from the Cotswolds and was worth upwards of 14s. a tod. Records state that some farmers owned thousands of sheep in the Fens, quite as large as flocks kept in Leicestershire, but many Fen farmers kept small flocks. The modest farmer kept a few sheep with two or three cows sharing grazings together.

A typical Fen farmer between 1530 and 1600 kept about six horses, four pigs, twenty sheep and ten cattle. An average of ten hens and a cockerel were kept on farms, these usually recorded in inventories as "pullen," which included ducks, geese and a few capons. Some assume quite wrongly that being a natural water shed for surrounding highland the Fens were bound to be desolate and for most part unproductive. Nothing is farther from the truth. For centuries the Fens did not even remotely approach poverty stricken regions and as early as 1334 the tax assessment per acre in the lowland was the fourth highest in the kingdom.

# 9. *Ague and Opium a bad mixture*

WRITING IN the nineteenth century, Canon Kingsley exclaimed: "Ah, well, at least we have wheat and mutton instead, and no more typhus and ague; and it is to be hoped, no more brandy drinking and opium eating; and children will live and not die."

His hopes were not immediately realised. Brandy drinking in the Fens continued, keeping up with the tendency in the rest of the country. Perhaps this had been introduced by our distant Scandinavian ancestors who excelled in "desperate drinking," and well they might after rowing their longships across the Fens relentlessly plagued by the area's stinging gnats. Fenmen resorted to a special vice of their own and ate opium. It was widely practised by the labouring classes and formed then an assiduous evil as indeed it does in many parts of the world in modern times. The drug's effect upon men, women and children reflected in their state of inanity, a not uncommon thing in rural areas which arose into the grossly exaggerated term of "senseless country bumpkins." The appearance of opium eaters betrayed them: they were wan and emaciate. Victims spent incredible amounts of money on the habit and by that they became desperately poor. In 1850 a poor family living in the Fens spent eight pence to ten pence a day for opium alone.

Once the opium habit had taken root the desire for larger amounts became irresistible and everyday necessities for the home sacrificed. The habit was handed down from father and mother to infants in the form of a concoction known as Godfrey's Cordial. When they were older, every day children were sent to the village shop for an extra pennyworth of opium. Yes! Shops actually sold the drug. Soon it became a habit to visit the shop several times a day to purchase the stuff. Eating opium was an old Fen practice and therefore considered quite acceptable by hapless victims and apothecaries alike. The latter believed that the drug relieved discomfort which arose from the ague, rheumatism and arthritis, common maladies of Fen districts. This was long before quinine was known. Thus opium, "the drug to relieve pain," easily persuaded patients to habitually resort to its use even when he or she were well. The drug's effect upon the brain gave victims the excuse of escaping temporarily from their daily problems, and introduced a stupor from which they were idenitified by those that knew no better as being village idiots. They literally experienced "trips," a form of excitement regarded by them as pleasurable second nature.

37

There is no conclusive evidence that eating opium in the Fen district arose from ague and related illnesses. Ague was an endemic, incommunicable disease, a paroxysmal fever. The cause of it was generally attributed to the "foggy" Fens, the extreme humidity of the air. This was introduced by the wet conditions underfoot giving rise to a noxious inhalation of moisture charged with decomposing organic substances, much the same as decomposing grass cuttings left for too long in a heap. It was observed that after a heavy rainfall, the land being lightly covered with water, the disease diminished. Anyone working near or on the water, such as bargemen, were worst affected by the ague or, to quote the locals, "Fen malaria." Some attributed it to ploughing the land after lying fallow for several years, which they said reintroduced the ague to local populations.

It was realised that anyone regularly living on a lower or ground floor, such as a cottage, tended to suffer from ague rather than people living on higher floors. Yet it was known that the poisonous vapours could be carried several hundred feet into the air. Ague did not only affect humans; horses, pigs, cows and dogs and cats were known to suffer from malarial diseases. The symptoms displayed in animals were different from those in humans, the latter quite capable of achieving notable longevity. Two hundred years ago it was not considered unusual if Fen people lived into their eighties and nineties. Wisbech, then with a population of 6,515 recorded three deaths which occurred between ninety and a hundred years of age. However, the unsalubrious fogs which covered the vast area were a marked testimony against any that might have harboured notions of going there to live "and many were fearful of entering the Fens of Cambridgeshire."

# HAZARDOUS JOURNIES IN THE LAND OF MISTS

In 1695, Celia Fiennes undertook a journey by horseback through England, an entertaining, revealing and sometimes dangerous experience. When she reached Stuntney she obtained her first view of the Fens. She looked across the ancient Causeway said to have been made by a monk for the safe passage of pilgrims (and others not always welcomed!) and observed that in winter the Causeway vanished beneath water and that the inhabitants at Ely and Stuntney "have no way but boates to pass in." Apparently Ely disgusted her. She wrote it was "the dirtiest place I ever saw, not a bitt of pitching in ye streets," except around the Palace and churches.

"It needs must be very unhealthy though the natives say to the contrary which proceeds from the customs and use, otherwise to persons born in up and dry countryes it must destroy them like rotton sheep and consumption and rhums." Gregory Leti in 1683 noted that "few people visit these districts who are not incommoded by fever, and the inhabitants are specially subject to it." Celia Fiennes pointed out that "the bishop does not care to stay long in this place not being for his health. They (the Fenmen) are a slothful people, and for little but ye taking care of their grounds and cattle which is of vast advantage. Where the yeares prove drye they gain so much that in case of six or seven wet yeares drove them all over, the one good yeare sufficiently repaires their loss."

She added that she ascended Ely cathedral's west tower and "could see Cambridge and a great prospect of the country what by reason of the great rains just before under water, all the fenny ground being all on a flat unless it be to one side of the town which is all high grounds into which they drive up their cattle to secure them in wet seasons." If Celia had tarried a little longer and perhaps travelled along the ridge to Little Downham, she would scarce conceal her amazement at the astonishing skil of the stilt walkers who ran very swiftly and their hands were free at all times. They tended hundreds of cattle and also vast flocks of sheep. She might have seen one man with his little son on stilts tending to no less than four hundred cattle. Hardly slothful people, Celia.

Casaubon, a friend of Bishop Andrew of Ely, suitably impressed at the age of Downham's inhabitants, wrote: "It is quite common to see here men who are *over* a hundred years old and one-hundred-and-twenty years old. I myself saw men over eighty and eighty-five years, strong in body and able to work in the fields." All that despite the ague! But one-hundred-and-twenty? Well . . .

*The moory soil, the wat'ry atmosphere,*
*With damp, unhealthy moisture chills the air.*
*Thick, stinking fogs and noxious vapours fall,*
*Agues and coughs are epidemical;*
*Hence every face presented to our view*
*Looks of a pallid or a sallid hue.*


Mr. Defoe and not a few visitors to the Fens for various reasons "longed to be delivered from the fogs and stagnant air." John Carey's *"New and Correct English Atlas"* published in 1787 makes many references to those conditions. While touring Cambridgeshire he observed: "In the Isle of Ely the air is damp, foul and unwholesome, but in the south east parts of this country is more pure and sallubrious"; of Norfolk: "The marshy and watery places are aguish and unwholesome"; and Huntingdonshire: "The air in some parts is thick and foggy, yet wholesome." One almost hears Fen Bill of Kyme Low Fen muttering: "Nothing more than a good Fenma expects. If you obtain a good living off the fen with almost everything to hand without asking, and with little or nothing to pay, there is bound to be a price of a different nature." One supposes that the summer months improved all this, but no sooner had the fogs lifted did another trial begin. A new and oppressive burden descended upon the people's skin – the annual infestation of super stinging gnats which remorsely fed off them day and night. A visitor, plagued by the pests, wearily entered in his diary: "As to the country about here, 'tis the most disagreeable I ever saw."

The midges and gnats in some places were exceedingly troublesome and some people "used nets made of silk to save them from being bitten at night." The hardy Fen speciality, ague, "was very rife, few strangers escaping without a seasoning." All around the Fens especially in Huntingdonshire there were "awful reservoirs of stagnated water which poisons the circumambient air for many miles about, and sickens and destroys many of the inhabitamts, especially such as are not natives. The ague, wrote one correspondent during the last century, was a distressful sickness, the people attacked by shiverings and pain in the limbs. When these symptoms abated, fever and thirst followed. For these reasons opium eating for medicinal purposes was common in the Fens. Opium was regarded as an antidote to the effect of obnoxious vapours. Chewing it was believed by many to be a necessity, and it was readily noticeable that if one stood in a druggist's shop on a market day it was commonplace to see "many a farmer's wife and many a rustic labourer enter and lay down their pence for a small packet of opium."

Thankfully, with the advent of modern drainage systems the ague disappeared, but prior to such improvements few fen families escaped its onslaught and many suffered from it throughout the year. It was noted that ague was at its worst in the Fens, but it also occurred along the Thames outfall in Essex and Kent and in Romsey Marsh. Consistent outbreaks occurred along the River Humber outfall and the Norfolk Broads. At all these places could be found stagnant water and marsh.

During drainage work in the seventeenth and eighteenth centuries, stories were heard of the anguish among Fen inhabitants complaining that the new work had literally stirred up diseases associated with marshy regions. When the drainage had at last been completcd and the muddy surface converted to virile soil, agues and associated disease virtually disappeared. "Malarial diseases (in the Fens), formerly so common, especially among the labouring population, has been reduced almost to nihility." *Fenland, Past and Present* (S. H. Miller and S. B. J. Skertchly).

Anyone traversing the Fens by road or by rail, walking, cycling, even observing the vast flatness from a 'plane, must think of the challenge and hardship experienced by its peoples in centuries gone by. Here was so much good in the sight of nature at her best and provident, and so much bad

seen in her worst moods – flood upon flood, destruction of human life, o
animals and property, of businesses. Could any other region in the countr
devastate mens efforts so thoroughly as did the Fens through rampagin
seas and freshwater, the damp "rhumy" mists, howling wind, thunder an
lightning, dreaded waterspouts, and repeated deadly visitations. Through a
this the Fen people braced themselves and rebuilt their lives and homes tim
and time again.

> The patient Fenman, who endur'd long time
> The various hardships of the watr'y clime;
> Whose slaught'ring gun and faithful dog has fed
> His wife and little family with bread;
> Now holds the plough, turns up the moory soil,
> And finds a vast increase reward his toil.
> His fields are cropt with diff'rent sorts of grain,
> His sheep and oxen graze the cheerful plain.

Even so, the floods still came and poured over the reclaimed grounds
The Fenmen . . .

> Betake them to their oars and safely row
> Over the very lands they us'd to plow.

Perhaps reminiscently, if not happily, the man of marsh and so
polished his oars, greased the great punt gun and took him to the shallow
sheltered by the reed fringed shore:

> And listens to the wild fowls distant quack;
> At dusk steers homeward with a plenteous freight,
> The crazy vessel groans beneath the weight.
> A tidy housewife waits his coming home,
> Gets dry apparel and cleans up her room.
> Prepared a cheerful fire, brings out her hoard
> And spreads a homely plenty o'er his board.
> To vend her fowl the dearest marts she tries,
> And with the profits household want supplies.
> The capitals' ev'n feasted with his store,
> And London carriers whistle at his door.
> Thus amply he his family maintains,
> And of his change of fortune scarce complains.
> His varied scenes of life now make him see:
> Nothing is certain, but uncertainty.

*Ely Cathedral seen from the Great River Ouse   (R. Farren 1883)*

Roots exposed by peat shrinkage: Feltwell Fen          T. A. Bevis

Shrinkage of peat in the Fens can cause odd sights like
that seen above: tree roots exposed above the surface which continues
to shrink.  In some places the concrete foundations of Georgian and
Victorian houses were exposed so much that steps were later
added to gain access.  The problems created by peat shrinkage is
visible on undulating roads and will be seen from some river banks,
the outlying land having receded several feet below river level.
Many brick buildings collapsed in the past two centuries and
some developed tendencies to lean, a particular example seen at
Benwick, near March.  Some church towers, too, tend to lean,
i.e., at Surfleet, Lincolnshire, and at Friday Bridge, Cambridgeshire,
where the steeple has actually dragged the church to one side.
A few Victorian towers and at least one church had to be demolished
but a great many medieval steeples and churches have survived.

# 10.   *A clergyman*
## *observes . . .*

REPRODUCED ON the concluding pages is a rare poem about the Fens, printed in Fenland Notes and Queries towards the end of the nineteenth century. It was written by an observant clergyman who, due to his calling to instruct his parishioners in religious matters, explained that he had very small opportunities to learn about the hard life of Fen people.

Commenting on great earth banks erected to prevent flooding he pointed out that "on those banks the inhabitants for their better security erect their miserable dwellings at a great distance from each other, and very remote from their parish churches to which they rarely resort, unless to a wedding, a christening, or a burying. So that they seem to be cut off from the community and are deprived of almost every advantage of social life. It is a rare thing to meet with a village of twenty houses together, unless in their towns from which they are many miles distant. They are, therefore, excluded from every opportunity of the very lowest education, and few of them arrive at higher erudition than to be able to read and write."

In his poem the author lauds the commendable fortitude, patience and resignation so characteristic of the old-time Fenmen. No men had more frequent occasion to submit themselves to the absolute disposal of Providence.

"To an upland farmer, the loss of his flock, or the failure of his crop, may be repaired by another more kindly season; but a drowned year strips the poor Fenman of every convenience of life. His all is gone. He is compelled to abandon his dwelling, and has not an inch of dry land to set foot on."

The numbers preceding certain lines of the poem relate to interesting and helpful notes found on other pages.

## THE INUNDATION OR THE LIFE OF A FENMAN

*Of sudden floods descending on the plain,*
*Which threat to drown a sinful land again,*
*Whose swelling surge with unresisted sway,*
*The lowly cot and cattle sweeps away,*
*Sing, heavenly CLIO, thou that did'st inspire*
*Thy fav'rit NASO with poetic fire;*

Assist my weak endeavours to pursue
The similar tale, amd make his fable true,
And as thou mov'd the Grecian bard to write
10    Of frogs embattl'd for the bloody fight,
Strengthen the efforts of my trembling pen
To celebrate an humble race of men,
Alike amphibious, by kind Nature's hand
Form'd to exist on water or on land.

15    The glorious sun, bright regent of the day,
For five dry seasons with his sultry ray,
Had warmed the earth, and in diurnal round,
Exhaled the vapours from the fenny ground;
The lessening flood relinquishes the strand,
20    And laughing CERES repossess'd the land.
As Nature kindly had performed her part,
She meets assistance from her handmaid art.
The banks are heighten'd, proper engines force
Th' expanded waters to their usual course.
25    The swampy bog now yields luxuriant grain,
And yellow harvests glad the low-land swain.

The patient FENMAN, who endur'd long time
The various hardships of the wat'ry clime,
Whose slaught'ring gun and faithful dog had fed
30    His wife and little family with bread,
Now holds the plough, turns up the moory soil,
And finds a vast increase reward his toil.
His fields are cropt with diff'rent sorts of grain,
His sheep and oxen graze the cheerful plain.
35    He sees himself completely happy now,
And calm content sits smiling on his brow.

But when frail Fortune smiles, and goods increase,
Our pride and vanity keep equal pace.
He feels th' effects of more propitious climes,
40    And now his prospects alter with the times.
His little hut, which by the bankside stood,
Cover'd with coat of sedge, the walls of mud,
Where each domestic use one room supplies,
His victuals here he dresses, here he lies:
45    A little lattice to let in the day,
With half extinguish'd light and glimm'ring ray,

Appears contemptuous in his loftier eye,
And much too streighten'd for his family,
He builds a handsom box on purchas'd ground,
His fields and pastures lie contiguous round,
The neighb'ring hinds admiring as they pass
The red-brick'd front, the sashes glitt'ring glass.
Barns, yards, conveniences of ev'ry kind,
A useful garden shelter'd from the wind,
Hogs in the stye and pullets at the door,
And ducks and geese and turkeys, many a score.

Our troubles with our affluence increase,
Plagued with too much, and yet displeas'd with less.
His barns are now too little to contain
The plenteous produce of his annual grain.
He builds them larger, and contrives more room,
To hoard his good and fruit for years to come.
Like the rich fool, to himself he fondly says,
"Be merry, eat and drink, and take thine ease."

What is all earthly bliss like infant's toys?
How vain our hopes; how fleeting are our joys!
The hour we think our happiness compleat,
The scene's reversed, and we lament our fate.

For now rough winter comes, the welkin low'rs,
Pregnant with boist'rous storms and frequent show'rs,
The south wind rises on her madid wings,
And the low hov'ring clouds together brings,
As at the deluge forty days and nights
The rain descended from the mountain's heights,
As all the fountains of the deep broke forth,
And heaven's windows op'd to drown the earth;
So now three wat'ry moons' incessant rain,
Came pouring down upon the marshy plain.
From all the neighb'ring hills the torrents glide
And meet the influx of the foaming tide.
Waves roll'd on waves accumulated rise,
And intermix their waters with the skies.
The stoutest banks in vain oppose their force,
In vain the art of man repels their course.
A breach at last is made, the currents pour
Thro' the deep chasm with tremendous roar.

Th' alarm'd inhabitants desert their home,
Whilst around their dwellings raging billows foam,
Betake them to their oars, and safely row
90      Over those very lands they us'd to plow.
Far as the wide horizons bounds the plain,

NEPTUNE extends his watery domain.
'Twixt land and wave the diff'rence is no more,
All is an open sea without a shore.
95      A vast expanse, beyond what eye can ken,
From Ely's lofty tow'rs to Lincoln fen.

There the fam'd abbey strikes the gazer's sight,
At once with pleasing horror and delight,
The mighty ruins, mould'ring walls, express
100     The ancient grandeur of this sacred place.
"Where CROWLAND, are thy domes, thy stately tow'rs?

"The rust of time thy priestly pride devours,
"Thy broken columns clasping ivy twines,
"And rev'rend moss surrounds thy mangled shrines.
105     "Where the loud organ charm'd the tuneful choir,
"The hooting owl and ominous bat retire."

Built and endow'd by MERCIA'S princely hand,
The pamper'd Abbot fixes here his stand,
To riot on the fatness of the land.
110     Where verdant pastures once were wont to feed
The fine-fleec'd sheep and ox of largest breed;

Where rapid rivers yield the fishy prey,
To fast delicious on each maigre day.
But seasons change, the soil so rich before,
115     By frequent inundation's render'd poor.
The country's desolate, the people fled,

And in a safer climate seek their bread.
The rushing waters cover all the plain,
And the sea re-assumes her own again.
120     Devouring pyke o'er flow'ry meadows stray,
Where sportive lambkins us'd to frisk and play.
The timorous hare, when all appear'd a sea,
Anxious for life, sits squat upon a tree.

45

The partridge, tir'd with flight, is glad to drop
Her wearied wings upon a willow top.
No living thing appears, but all is lost,

Or driven from th' inhospitable coast.
"Unhappy clime! malignant air dispense,
O'er thy devoted head their influence.
"Ev'n when rich plenty smiles upon thee most,
The moory soil, the wat'ry atmosphere,

With damp, unhealthy moisture chills the air.
Thick, stinking fogs, and noxious vapours fall,
Agues and coughs are epidemical.
Hence ev'ry face presented to our view,

Looks of a pallid or a sallow hue.
Nor kindliest seasons these complaints redress,
They're owing to the GENIUS of the place.
Near to the bank, in a dark dismal hut,
Made of the stern of an old shatter'd boat,

Pale FEBRIS  sat - her shrivel'd aspect shows
A shocking sense of sickness, pain and woes;
She shiver'd o'er a cow-dung's smoaky fire,
Squallied her looks and wretched her attire,
An old blue cloak was o'er her shoulders flung,

Her patched and tatter'd garment round her hung,
Her hollow eyes with scalding rheum look'd red,
And quiv'ring palsey shook her bending head;
Catarrhs and intermittings with her dwell,
And such the poison of her loathsom cell,

Whene'er she stirs abroad she taints the ground,
And spreads the direful pestilence around.
But her Fen hero her attacks defies,
Healthy by temp'rance and by exercise.
From early infancy to manhood's prime,

His constitution weathers with the clime,
But times and seasons are in God's own pow'r,
He must submit, and waits the approaching hour.

46

160       For now the BITTERN undulates her note,
Like a deep-mouth'd bassoon, and swells her throat.
The screaming seamows hover o'er the plain,
Portentous signs of gath'ring storms and rain.
He sees the coming flood, he hears the wind,
165      And meets his fate with a determn'd mind.
The sudden deluge overflows his ground,

And his fine stock is either starv'd or drown'd.
His barns, wherein his choicest grain he stores,
Let in the water at the folding doors,
170      His corn ricks are half drowned to the top,
Which like a SYPHON sucks the liquor up.

His stacks of hay are swimming o'er the mead,
Useless to him, his cattle want no feed.
At last his mansion, whose unusual load,
175      Ill suited to the soil whereon it stood,
The waters sapping the foundation round,

Falls an unwieldy ruin to the ground.
Whilst his deserted cot the storm derides,
And stands superior to the swelling tides.
180      He sees an end of all his toil and pain,
And hastens to his little hut again.

Renews his former life, and gets afloat,
With gun and spaniel in his cockle boat.
He rises early, and he late takes rest,
185      And sails intrepid o'er the wat'ry waste;
Waits the return of  Shot-seal on the lake,

And listens to the wild fowls distant quack,
At dusk steers homeward with a plenteous freight,
The crazy vessel groans beneath the weight,
19      A tidy house-wife waits his coming home,
Gets dry apparel and cleans up her room.

Prepares a cheerful fire, brings out her hoard,
And spreads a homely plenty o'er his board.
To vend her fowl the dearest marts she tries,
195      And with the profit household wants supplies.
The capital's ev'n feasted with his store,

And London carriers whistle at his door.
Thus amply he his family maintains,
And of his change of fortune scarce complains.
*200*      His varied scenes of life now make him see,
Nothing is certain, but uncertainty.

That anxious fears attend our happiest state,
And greater grow as we are growing great.
That who with higher affluence is blest,
*205*      Dreads more the loss of what he is possest.
That he alone is out of fortune's pow'r,

Who sunk so low that he can sink no low'r.
And who's life comforts without pain would share,
Must very little have to hope or fear.
*210*      That cares and crosses every soul oppress,
And who with patience bears them, makes them less.

That God's wise providence our lot hath thrown,
And the disposal of it is his own.
*215*      He once indeed was rich, and now he's poor,
But yet he is but what he was before.
And all his interval of plenty seems,
As airy visions and delusive dreams.

## FINIS

The unnamed poet wrote at an undisclosed time. His manner is in the tyle of Milton, Ovid, Horace or Virgil. Certain lines will be of interest to eaders and these are given as up-dated notes. The original notes ccompanied the poem when it was first published.

*Line 27 - The patient Fenman, etc.:* The Fenman was compared to the American Red Indian. The latter had a much preferable life to that of the 1an of the Fens. They both lived by their gun; the Red Indian traversed the voods and mountains in search of food and retired to a warm tent or cabin. 'he Fenman went out in a little skiff, which a puff of wind would overset, nd paddled the water until sunset, returning to his miserable hut wet and old. Both were skilled fishermen and took with them their favourite dog.

*52 - The red-brick'd front, the sashes' glitt'ring glass:* The whole haracter is realised in John Leaford, a Fenman of yesteryear. He was a 1bourer in the fen, and was known to be a banker. When the land was looded he provided for his family in the custom of the Fens, by killing wild owl. Leaford was employed by the corporation of Adventurers in making

48

and repairing earth banks. This labourer obtained money, purchased Adventurers' lands at an advantageous price and, by a happy succession of dry seasons, grew very rich. He built a fine brick and sashed house near the bank of the Hundred Foot at Oxlode in the parish of Little Downham Isle of Ely. This house in a better district would well deserve the name of a hall and be suitable as a dwelling for a rural squire. John Leaford was employed as an officer under the Corporation and at last realised his ambition and became a conservator. Not surprisingly he was perfectly illiterate, but this was seen as an advantage. If his bills for works done by order of the Board passed favourably, it was very well; if they were objected to, Leaford screened himself by declaring it was the fault of his translator, for he could neither read nor write.

*101 - Where, Crowland, are thy domes, etc.:* The reader will excuse this digression when he reflects that it is designed as a compliment to the Fen country, in recollecting the many noble religious foundations which have formerly adorned it. After all, did not the Saxon race call the Fen "The Holy Land of the English"? Shouldham, Marham, Pentney and Wormegay abbeys in Norfolk; Ramsey abbey in the fens of Huntingdonshir which was possessed of vast lordships and estates in Norfolk. In the Fen of Lincolnshire, Swineshead and Crowland; and not forgetting Thorney, Ely Outwell and Chatteris in the south Fens.

*107 - Built and endow'd by Mercia's princely hand:* Crowland abbe was built by Ethelbald, King of Mercia, at vast expense. This religiou foundation was set upon a morass and the builders were obliged to driv down strong piles of oak to support the noble superstructure. It was als largely endowed by the King. What little remains of this famous abbey i impressive and serves now as the parish church.

*111 - The fine-fleec'd sheep, and ox of largest breed:* The sheep o Lincolnshire were remarkable for the fineness of their wool, and large herd of cattle were bred in that county.

*222 - The timorous hare, etc.:* The hare and a partridge seeking th security of a tree may seem extraordinary, but it is said that it actuall happened at Salter's Lode near Downham Market. A large tract of lan there kept dry for the owner for a month when all the adjacent country wa drowned, occasioned the little game in that district to resort thither i order to forage for food and gain security from the floods. However, storm arising from the north-west caused the banks to collapse and th water poured through. In no time the dry land was utterly inundated People employed to remove the stock from the ground took a hare and partridge alive from the top of a willow tree.

*174 - At last his mansion, etc.:* The fen being a morass, and tha newly drained will not support a foundation of brick and stone. This i readily seen in some buildings which lean out of true, such as a house a

Benwick, and some church towers notably those at Surfleet, Lincolnshire and Friday Bridge, Cambridgeshire. A few towers were demolished to prevent the church buildings from being pulled over and at least one church in the area, that at Benwick, as a result of shifting foundations had to be entirely demolished. More than a hundred years ago many leaning houses could be seen in the Fens, particularly one at Mepal bridge in the Isle of Ely which took on a glow of fame. It was formerly the mansion seat of Captain Fortree, and was built of stud work and turf between instead of brick for lightness. It was said to be an elegant building with ornaments of stucco, a handsome walled-in court yard, and gardens walled-in at the rear. Yet still it fell victim to subsidence.

*183 – With gun and spaniel in his cockle boat:* This was called a gunning boat not much longer than the gun it contained, which was made of great length to kill at a vast distance. The boat was constructed very light, that the Fenman might easily haul it over the bank when he wanted to sail into other waters in search of fowl. It was propelled by short paddles so as not to create ripples. In a brisk gale it danced like a cockle shell upon the waves.

*186 – Waits the return of shot-seal on the lake:* This term was used in the Fen country to denote the time – about sunset – when the wildfowl returned from sea (which they were said to fly to every day) into the fresh waters. In the old-time Fen language, lake was an open part of the river or the waters in the fen, when a hard frost sets in, in a drowned year, to which the wildfowl resorted for food. A mere was sometimes called a lake. Although generally of a shallow depth these expanses of water could be dangerous, especially in the event of sudden squalls or gales. Many Fenmen and their families were known to drown on such occasions. Ramsey Mere and Ugg Mere were particularly notorious for loss of human life.

*197 – And London carriers whistle at his door:* As an instance of the luxury of the metropolis, there was a number of people known as kedgers who, when the Fens could be travelled over, called regularly at the Fenmen's houses to buy fish and fowl at not immoderate prices. They would send them to town by the butter boats, or sell them to the higglers employed on London markets. But that was considered to be no great inconvenience when compared to Norwich weavers who sent special messengers from that city to Caxton which is almost one hundred miles, to meet the north country carriers with fresh salmon!

*198 – Thus amply he his family maintains:* It is incredible to believe what great advantage the skilful Fenman made of his winter shooting in a drowned year, and in the following summer of his fish. By the overflowing of Whittlesey Mere and other great reservoirs of fish the whole of the country was plentifully stocked with them. By all accounts the rough clad, illiterate Fenman was by no means a poor soul.

Dressed for the kill — a Fen "Slodger" 1895

# Characters of Fen and Mere

The Fen gunners, a tough race of water men, usually built their own vessels. When used regularly the punt guns were devastatingly effective, but if a gun had been stored up for long periods it might deteriorate. It was known for a charge of powder to be left in the barrel and it had hardened. If a gun had seen long service – some were over a hundred years old – there was a great risk of old hardened powder igniting and forcing its way through the sides of the barrel rather than along it.

When triggered, if the gun "sang like a kettle" without actually discharging, the gunner hastily ejected himself from the vessel and, if he could, sought the protection of the earth bank or risk being blown up. The guns were ponderous things and took a lot of lugging over the marsh. Like all firearms they had to be kept meticulously clean and as dry as possible.

An old Fenman spoke of the day he lined up his gun on Mepal wash and knocked the daylight from 160 wigeon at the cost of only six shots. This man claimed his best shot ended the lives of 53 peewits, and to top it all he took 48 wigeon with one big bang from his punt gun. It was an education observing a punt-gunner creeping stealthily towards his victims. The gun, more like a cannon, was fixed to the front of the vessel and the gunner occupied a horizontal position behind the breech. He aimed the punt at the group of feeding wildfowl and his approach was patiently stealthy, an inch at a time, taking advantage of any protective sedge. The vessel was propelled by short paddles held deep in the water by the gunner, so as to cause no tell-tale ripples upon the surface,

There were several such men living from the feathered produce of the Fens. The old Fen Slodgers armed with long, hooked poles were succeeded by the punt gunner with his murderous blast of shot. In turn he gave away to the wild-fowler and his double-barrelled shotgun.

T. Bevis

# FEN PROVINCIALISMS

## "A"

AEGAR, HIGRE – A dangerous and violent tide in some rivers

AN ALL – Also

AS YET – "I can't help you as yet"

ASH KEYS – Seed vessels of an ash tree

AX'D OUT – The marriage banns

ARSY VARSY – Vive versa.

## "B"

BACK'S UP – Someone who is offended

BACK AN' EDGE – Completely, entirely

BARE BUBBLING – Unfledged

BAIT (TO) – To rest a horse

BESLINGS – The first milk from a cow after calving

BLEB – A bubble, blister

BLEE – Open, bleak fen

BORN DAYS – A lifetime; "I never heard of it in all my born days"

## "C"

CASELTY – Uncertain; "He's a caselty old fellow"

CESSES – Peat shaped into square blocks

COP – To throw; "Cop it over here"

CHARES – Odd jobs

CLUNG – Heavy; "The land is clung"

COPPLING – Unsteady; "The coppling stack will soon fall over"

COPPLE CROWNED – Tufted; "Look at that copple crowned bird"

CAG MAG – Inferior meat; Cagg Maggs: old and tough geese sent out of the Fens to London

CHELDY – Saucy

CHUNTER – To mutter

CORNED – The worse for drink

CHIMBLEY – Chimney

CHAMBLED – Parts of corn left by ▮ are chamblings

CAUVE – A bulge in a tank

CLINK – Smart; "She's looking clink"

CHAP MONEY – Money given back ▮ luck

CHECK CHECK – A call to pigs; "Chur▮ drive them away

CHIP-OUT – A quarrel

CLAGS – Dirty wool clipped off sheep

CLAT – A tell-tale; a gossiper was call▮ tell-clat

CLOW or CLOUGH – A flood gate, slui▮

CLUNCH – Blunt in manners; ▮ tempered

COLLOGUE – To conspire secretly

CREE – To boil gently

CRONE – An old, toothless sheep

CROODLE – To lie together for warmth

CULLINGS – Inferior stock

CUMBER GROUNDS – Applies to use▮ trees; ("Why cumbreth the ground?" ▮ 13, 7)

## "E"

EAT THE LEEK – To eat your own wo▮

EA, EAU – Water or drain; (though▮ originate from Scandinavia or Denmark)

EDDISH – The first growth of grass ▮ mowing

ELDERN – The elder tree

ESHUCK – A false link; temporary repa▮ chains

ENEW – Enough; "He's had enew"

## "F"

FAL-LAL – An idle tale.

FELL – Savage; a fierce dog

51

FELON - A whitlow, usually on the
finger; a disease in a cow's bag

FEN NIGHTINGALES - Frogs

FELZON - To fasten

FLEAK - A wattle hurdle

FLOOD O! - Exclamation term used by
bargemen at appearance of a tide in a
river

FLUSH - Even, level; "A flush of
money"

FOOTY - Small; "A footy little
penknife"

FRAME - Promise; "He frames well"

FRUMENTY - The fungus Lycopper-
on vovista

"G"

GAFFER - Master or foreman; a
corruption of grandfather

GALLUS - Mischievous

GAUBY - A lout or clown

GEE - An order to a horse to turn to
the right

GEN - Gave; "He gen it to me"

GERNE - To grin

GILLYVERS - Wallflowers

GIVE OVER - Cease, leave off

GNATTER - To grumble

GOFFER - A species of teacake, made
goffering irons

GO TO THE BAD - To fail in
business

GO TO GUYHIRN - A derisive
expression originating from the gibbet on
which the bodies of felons were suspended
at that Fen village

GOTE - An outlet of a drain or water
course

GOODLE - To flog

GOZZARD - A person in charge of
geese

GRIP - A small ditch

GULSH - Short and thick; gross

GUY - An ill-dressed person; derived
from Guy Fawkes

"H"

HAKING - Loitering; "A great haking
fellow"

HANDSEL - Luck money

HARROWED - Worn out

HASSOCK - Coarse grass; an order
dated December 24th, 1651 allowed any
private owner in the Fens to have his
land hassocked by Scottish prisoners-of-
war at six shillings to the acre

HAWBUCK - A raw, country lad

HAWM - To lounge about; "Don't
hawm about so"

HAZLE - First process of drying
washed linen

HEADACHE - The scarlet poppy

HEADLAND - The outside of a field
where horses (and tractors) turned

HEFT - A handle

HERNSHAW - The heron

HIGGER - A man who kept horses

HIGHTY-TIGHTY - Lighthearted

HIVES - Small risings on the skin

HOBBINGS - Hay so formed

HODDING SPADE - A special
implement used by dikers (or roders) in
the Fens

HODENDOD - The snail shell

HO-GO - A vile smell

HOLT - Plantation; "Down by the
willow holt"

HUMMER - A falsehood

HUNNY - To fondle

HURN - As in Guyhirn; a water
corner from "Gwy," an ancient word
meaning water; the Fen people of the
Saxon and post-Conquest eras were known
as water people; "land of the Gwywas"

## "I"

**ILL-THRIVEN** - Spoken of a delicate person.

**INGS** - Low lying meadows

**INQUIRATION** - An inquiry

## "J"

**JACK-ON-A-PINCH** - A temporary or make-shift worker

**JARZEN** - A donkey; "Boozing jarzen" - a drunken lout

**JENNY WISP** - Will-o'-the-Wisp; an ignited plume of marsh gas which moved about

**JIBBER** - A reluctant horse

**JOBBER** - A dealer in livestock

**JOSKIN** - A country clown

## "K"

**KEEPING ROOM** - A room usually occupied by the family

**KELL** - The loose fat of a pig

**KINDLE** - To bring forth young animals

**KISSING CRUST** - The over-running portion of a loaf of bread

**KITTLE** - "The cat has kittled"; bringing forth her young

**KO-UP** - "Come up"; a call for horses

## "L"

**LAPE** - To walk carelessly

**LAP-UP** - To wrap up well

**LEATHER-HEAD** - A stupid person

**LEAD** - Eel trap

**LESK** - The groin or flank; peculiar to Lincolnshire

**LIGHTS** - The lungs; "The sheep's lights were half diseased"

**LIKEN** - In danger of; likely

**LIMB** - A child of mischievous habi

**LISSOME** - Nimble, active; Said of slow fellow, "He's lissome as a cow cri

**LODE** - A fen drain

**LOWANCE** - Allowance

**LURCHER** - A crossbred dog used f catching hares

## "M"

**MALEHACK** - To carve me awkwardly

**MAM, MAMMY** - Mother; opposite Dad (father); of early British origin

**MANAGEMENT** - Chemical or artific manure

**MATTLE** - To match; "They do mattle"

**MASTER** - Husband; used by wife

**MAUL** - A hedger's tool; also to ma dirty; ill-treated

**MAVIS** - The missel thrush

**MAY-BEE** - The cockchafer

**MEALY-MOUTHED** - Afraid speaking plainly

**MERE** - A sheet of water, common the fen region in pre-drainage times

**MISSUS** - Wife; used by the husbar

**MIZZLE** - Small rain

**MUCHER** - Of much account; "He's a mucher"

**MULFERED** - Worn with fatigue

**MUN** - Must

**MYSEN** - Myself

## "N"

**NAB** - To seize; from Danish "napp

**NAIL-PASSER** - A gimlet, used making holes for nails and screws

**'NATIONLY** - Very; "She's nat cross"

**NAPPERS** - Knees; "He's down on nappers

**NATTERAL** – A kind, simple person
**NAUTHIN** – Nothing; generally Norfolk
**NAVVIES** – Excavators in the Fens; ormerly river bankers
**NEW BEARD** – A cow that has ecently calved
**NIGH-HAND** – Most likely
**NINE-CORNS** – A pipe of tobacco
**NINES** – Perfection; "It's nines"
**NISTE** – Nice
**NOAH'S ARK** – A formation of cloud aid to resemble a boat, and to be a sign f rain
**NOBBUT** – Naught but
**NO NATION PLACE** – An out-of-the-ay place; there were several in the ens
**NOUS** – Sense, knowledge; (Greek)
**NOWT** – Nothing

## "O"

**OCHRE** – Money, especially gold
**ODS RITIKINS** – A form of oath
**ODLING** – Without equal
**OLLANDS** – Grazed, seed or clover own lands
**ONMOST** – Almost; "omast"
**ON TEN TOES** – Afoot
**OOKER** – A speaker who exaggerates
**OUT-ASKED** – The final publishing of e marriage banns
**OUTNER** – A stranger; foreigner
**OVERSET** – To recover from an illness; he has overset the ague"
**OWLEY** – Filthy
**OWT** – Anything; "Is there owt in hat she says"

## "P"

**PAD THE HOOF** – To travel on foot
**PAM IN HAND** – The knave of clubs

**PAMMY** – A thick, soft hand
**PASH** – Something rotten
**PELT** – The skin
**PICKLE** – A miserable condition
**PIE, PYE** – A round stack of mustard
**PIG-CHEER** – Sausages
**PIG-HEADED** – Stubborn
**PILGAR** – A spear to catch eels with
**PINK** – The chaffinch
**PLASH** – To lay a hedge
**PLOUGH BULLOCKS** – Plough boys going from house to house on Plough Monday
**PLUCK** – A crow; to pick a quarrel
**POKE** – A big sack
**POPPLE** – The poplar tree
**POTHER** – Bustling about; "What's all the pother about, then?"
**POTATO-TRAP** – The mouth
**PRECIOUS** – An ironical superlative; "A precious mess he got me into"
**PRIMP** – Privet
**PUDGE** – A little puddle of water
**PUFF-THE-DART** – A game played in public houses for beer
**PULK** – A coward
**PYE-BACK** – Carried pick-a-back
**PYKELET** – Round cakes

## "Q"

**QUACKEN** – To choke, suffocate
**QUAG** – A swamp; from quagmire
**QUALITY** – The gentry
**QUARTER ILL** – Cattle disease: black leg (gangrenous fever)
**QUERPO** – Stripped of upper garments
**QUICK STICKS** – Immediately
**QUILT** – To beat; "I'll quilt you"

## "R"

**RABBIT IT** – A petty oath

**RACK-A-PELT** – A troublesome fellow

**RACK UP** – The last food given to horses at night

**RAFTY** – Fusty, rancid

**RAKE** – To wander; applied to cattle that will not settle

**RAMPER** – A raised road; probably from rampart; there are several in the Fens, usually surmounting river banks

**RAP STICK** – Device for sharpening scythes

**RAWP** – To shout; "Don't rawp so"

**REASTY** – Rancid; applied to bacon

**RED-ROW** – A stage in ripening barley

**REED-SHOFE** – A sheaf of reed

**REMBLE** – To change places

**RENCH** – To rinse

**RERE** – Meat, half cooked

**REVERENCE** – The Fen clergy were usually addressed "Your Reverence"; thought to be introduced to the Fens by Irish workmen

**RIFF-RAFF** – Disorderly people; also a jumble of rubbish

**RIG-WELDED** – Said of sheep when thrown onto their backs

## "S"

**SNACK, SNECK** – The iron fastening for a door

**SNAPE, SPEAP** – To rebuke or correct sharply; "Snape him and teach him a lesson"

**SNASTE or SNATHE** – The burnt wick of a candle

**SNEERING MATCH** – A grinning match

**SNOW-REEK** – A drift of snow

**SOCK-DIKE** – A dike at the rear of a main drain

**SOGGER** – Anything big or heavy

**SOGGIE** – Said of a bullock full of flesh

**SOOL'EM, sOWL'EM** – To induce dog to fight or attack something

**SOSSING** – Mixing matter together to make a dirty mess

**SASSE** – A navigable sluice or lock

**SPIGHTLE** – A small grass paddock

**SPIT** – The depth of a spade when digging

**SPITTLE-STAFF** – A spud for stabbing up thistles

**SPORE** – Spared; left alive; "If I am spore I'll stay with you"

**SPRUNNY** – Neat, spruce; sweetheart

**SPOLSH** – Brittle through dryness

**SPURN** – A short post to prop up the lower end of a gatepost

· **SPRATCHED** – Of eggs cracked by chick; from Danish "spraken," cracked

**SQUAT** – Silent; "You should keep squat on this matter"

**SWIZZLE** – A mixed drink

**SWOUND** – To swoon

## "T"

**TACK** – Applies to unpalatable food "This is hard tack"

**TANTADLUM TART** – A tart in which the fruit is not covered by a crust

**TATER TRAP** – The mouth

**TED** – To pull hay together in small heaps

**TENISE** – A fine flour sieve

**TELL-CLAT** – A tale bearer

**TETCHY** – Peevish; hard to please

**THACK** – Thatch

**THICK** – Friendly

**THRUFF** – Through

**THUMB PIECE** – A meal of bread and cheese eaten when standing

**TIED** – Bound by a promise or agreement

**TIMES AND OFTEN** – Frequently

**TING-TANG** – A paltry, worthless article

**TIT** – A small light horse

**TOD** – Dung

**TOKE** – A simpleton

**TOMMY** – Provisions

**TOM-TOE** – The great toe

**TOP-UP** – To finish

**TOSHES** – Tusks

**TOSS-POT** – A drunkard

**TOTTERING** – A person recovering from an illness had "a totering time of it"

**TROTTLES** – Dung of sheep, hares or rabbits

**TRUCKLE-BED** – Obsolete article of furniture; also a hanger-on, a toady

**TURF** – Dutch word appropriate to the fens; in Ramsey Fen turves were called hassies

**TWANG** – A sharp, acute pain

**TWITCH** – Couch grass

## "U"

**UNDERLOUT** – Of cattle the weakest was thus called

**UNPOSSIBLE** – Impossible

**UP-TO-DICK** – Up to the mark

**UNSNECK** – Unfasten

**UVVERS** – Grass mown from the dykeside

**VENOM, VEMON** – Used as a verb, "It will venom you if you're not careful"

## "W"

**WADED** – Roded; cleansed from reads; labourers tidying dykes were called Roders; many attended to steam pumps and wind engines during winter

**WAFFLING** – Disagreeable; "He's a waffling fellow"

**WALL-EYED** – Applied to a horse with white eyes

**WALSH** – A lean-to building; attached to a barn

**WEATHER-BREEDER** – Too fine to last; farmers and their labourers were generally good at forecasting the weather, by observing plants and berries for instance and cloud cumulus of which there are many varieties; behaviour of animals was also noted and wind and temperature indicative of changing weather conditions

**WET YOUR WHISTLE** – Take light refreshment

**WHADDON ORGANS** – Frogs

**WHIG** – Buttermilk; in ancient times this was sometimes used to coat stone walls, such as churches, to encourage development of natural growth

**WHIM-WHAMS** – Fancies

**WHIRLIGIG** – Fan used to dress corn; wind-engine pumping water along drains

**WHITTERER** – Whinging; complaining

**WIND-A-BIT** – To halt; give breathing time

**WINDLE** – A snowdrift

**WINDING SHEET** – A film of carbon in a candle; it was held to presage a death in the family

**WIRE-IN** – Hurry to work

**WIZZEN STAKES** – Used to fasten sheaves of sedge at the top of banks

**WOOSH** – Ordering a horse to turn to the left

## "Y"

**YAFFLING** – "A little yaffling cur"

**YARD-OF-CLAY** – A churchwarden's clay pipe

**YELLOW BELLY** – A person born in the Lincolnshire Fens

# *Epilogue*

## IN PRAISE OF FEN AND MERE

It is no exaggeration to associate the Fens with accolades of prai poured upon places of outstanding beauty in England's green and pleasa land. "A very paradise and a heaven for the beauty and delight thereof . . penned one writer who saw the Fens in their natural cloak of colo according to the season. Famous authors, Stukely and Kingsley wrote glowing terms of the Fens. None can describe in better terms than did M Hissey in his book *"Over Fen and Wold"* published in 1898.

"A strange, weird world this English Fenland seems to unfamiliar eye especially when seen under a brooding sky; and there is a peculiar quality ·mystery that baffles description and cannot be analysed, in the deep blu grey palpitating gloom that gathers over the Fenland distances when they under the threatening shadow of some coming storm.

"Under such conditions the scenery of the Fens is pronouncing striking, but even under ordinary circumstances a man can have but lit poetry in his soul who cannot admire its wild beauties, its vast breadths luxuriant greenery over which the eye can range unrestrained for leagu upon leagues on every side, its space expressing distances and its migh cloudscapes, for the skyscape is a feature in the Fenland prospect not to overlooked. I am inclined to think that its sky scenery – if I may be allow the term – is the finest and most wonderful in the world.

"It is worth a long journey to the district if only to behold one of glorious sunsets, when you look upon a moist atmosphere saturated wi colour so that it becomes opalescent, and the sinking sun seen through t vibrating air is magnificent to twice its real size as it sets on a world melting rubies and molten gold. From the western shores of far-c California I have looked down upon the sun dipping into the wide Paci amidst a riot of colour, but nothing like this! It is not always necessary leave England in search for the strange and beautiful . . ."

*"I sing Floods muzzled and the Ocean tam'd, Luxurious Rivers govern'd and reclaim'c Waters and Banks confin'd as in a Gaol, Till kinder Sluices let them go on Bail Streams curb'd with Dammes like Bridles taught t' obey, And run as strait as if the saw their way."* (Attributed to Samuel Fortrey, 1685)

57

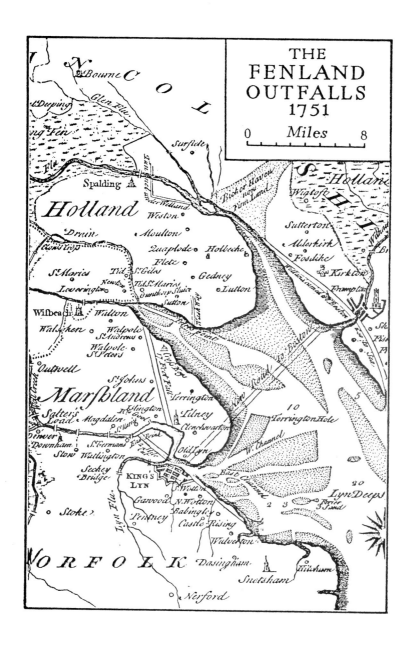

A section taken from "A Map of the Great Level of the Fens" in N. Kinderley's "The Ancient and Present State of the Navigation of the Towns of Lynn, Wisbeach, Spalding and Boston" (1751).

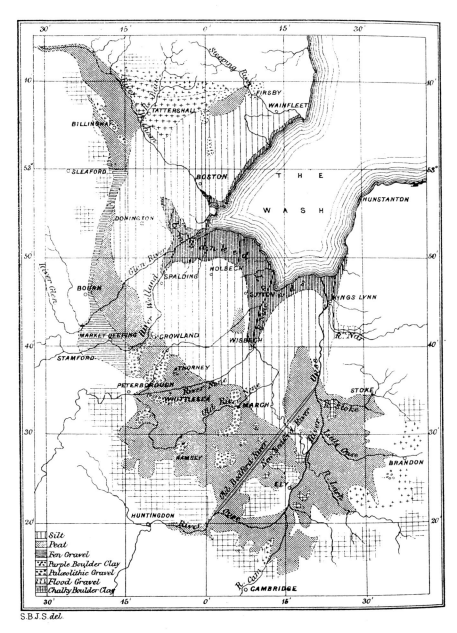

S.B.J.S. del.

*Geological map of the Fens showing deposits of clay,
gravel, peat and silt.*